VEGGIE LOVERS

Cook Book

by

Chef Morty Star

Foreword by Michael Klaper, M.D.

**GOLDEN
WEST ☼
PUBLISHERS**

Cover art by Kris Steele

Library of Congress Cataloging-in-Publication Data

Star, Morty, 1939—
    Veggie Lover's Cook Book / by Morty Star
    Includes Index.
    ISBN 0-914846-77-9
    1. Vegetarian cookery.   I. Title
TX837.S73   1994   94-1650
641.5'636—dc20   CIP

Printed in the United States of America on recycled paper.

Information in this book is deemed to be authentic and accurate by author and publisher. However, they disclaim any liability incurred in connection with the use of information appearing in this book.

Golden West Publishers, Inc.
4113 N. Longview Ave.
Phoenix, AZ 85014, USA

(602) 265-4392

Dedication

To all vegetarians who have been willing to take a stand, lead the way, inspire others and keep the vision of a healthier, peaceful world.

Acknowledgements

To all my friends and teachers in vegetarian communities and organizations who have inspired me and made a significant impact in my quest for health.

To my sponsors in the health food and housewares industries whose contributions have made our seminars and cooking classes possible.

To Norma Jean, my soul mate and partner, who has brought love, joy, balance and support into my life.

Table of Contents

BREAKFASTS

SOUPS & SANDWICHES

SALADS & DRESSINGS

SAUCES, GRAVIES, SPREADS & DIPS

Cooking Guidelines

The following are a few of the basic guidelines when cooking some of the most popular beans and legumes. The soaking time of beans should be followed as per package instructions. Water level in cooking beans should be approximately three parts water to one part beans.

Soybeans should be cooked for about 2 1/2 - 3 hours. Garbanzo, kidney, red beans, adzuke beans should be cooked for 1 - 1 1/2 hours. Split peas, lentils, lima beans should be cooked for 45-55 minutes.

Vegetables are best when they are soft and tender. Therefore, it is important to check vegetables during the steaming process as cooking times will vary according to the size and cuts of the vegetables. Be sure to save the juices for other cooking recipes calling for vegetable stock.

Carrots, brussels sprouts, cabbage, eggplant, onions, squash, zucchini 10-13 minutes. Beets, cauliflower 15-20 minutes.
*****
Vegetable stock is made from the juices of vegetables or cooked with water. Most of the vegetable stock I use in my recipes comes from steamed vegetables.

Introduction

I am Chef Morty Star and I have been a vegetarian for almost 25 years. I am the creator and president of *Journey Into Health*. *Journey Into Health* is a vehicle for me and other vegetarians to spread the word regarding health.

My own vegetarian journey has been cleansing, healing and delicious. I've travelled the U.S.A., Mexico and Jamaica studying various vegetarian diets.

After spending years experimenting with sprout diets, fruitarian diets, raw food diets and juice regimens, my journey has led me ultimately to a delicious, nutritious diet that includes grains, legumes, vegetables and fruits.

In addition to my commitment to a pure vegetarian diet, I feel passionately about ending the killing of animals. Doctors, scientists and even the U.S. government have begun an avalanche of news releases recently stating that people must lower their consumption of animal fats.

The U.S. government now says the four food groups we learned in school are not based on a healthy diet. We do not need meat or dairy in our diets. A diet of grains, legumes, vegetables and fruits fill all of our daily dietary needs.

Doctors are finally saying that most of our debilitating illnesses today are caused by bad diet. What is "bad diet"? "Bad diet" is too much animal fat! When I began my vegetarian journey 25 years ago, I was considered a pioneer. It was hard making my own meat and dairy substitutes out of grains and legumes.

It is very exciting to me today to find our health food stores and supermarkets stocking so many health conscious (no animal products) choices in all varieties of foods. The future looks a whole lot brighter to me as I see more and more people each day becoming more aware in their eating and their health.

As a vegetarian, you will experience more energy, your thoughts will be clearer and you will experience a greater amount of compassion for your planet. My goal is to "turn you on" to delicious, fun new foods. Foods for the future and for your pleasure now.

Because we humans are such social animals and we have our cravings, I have found substitute flavors and textures that will satisfy your taste buds. I do love my food and I say you will, too!

Chef Morty Star

Foreword

Until recent years, the food on our tables was primarily served to appease our hunger and please our palate. Rich meats, heavy cream sauces and dairy-laden desserts were the rule for a "complete meal" and a portly girth was accepted as a sign of one who "really enjoyed his food". Today's perspective, however, reveals to us that the food we eat holds a far greater importance than mere taste, both as a creator of health or disease, as well as a powerful shaping force upon our environment.

Food and Health

Recent medical evidence[1] clearly shows that our high fat dietary style of the last 50 years has been a recipe for disaster for our health. The Standard American Diet (S.A.D.), which can include bacon and eggs for breakfast, a cheeseburger for lunch, cheese and sausage pizza for dinner and ice cream for dessert, sends tides of animal fat surging through our bloodstream every four hours, leading to innumerable health catastrophes. Such a high-fat dietary style has been implicated in the current health epidemics of obesity, high blood pressure, adult-onset diabetes, clogged arteries leading to heart attacks and strokes, as well as several common cancers[2-7].

In contrast, a study has been made comparing those who follow the S.A.D. with those in countries in Asia, Africa and South America who continue to follow their traditional diet based upon grains, legumes, fruits and vegetables. Those in the latter category are typically lean and healthy with normal blood pressure, healthful cholesterol levels and far lower incidence of the degenerative diseases that plague most North Americans.

The reason for these differences in national health are fairly apparent when one considers differences in diet. Cholesterol is found only in meats, dairy and other animal products. No plant food contains cholesterol, so one can consume ample portions of grains, cereals, breads and potatoes, along with tasty fruits and vegetables with delicious sauces, and still become lean and light

(See References - Page 126)

with clean arteries and abundant vitality. It is these nutritional realities that make Chef Star's pure and healthy vegetarian cookbook so valuable.

The following recipes are filled with hearty meals, fit for beginning diner or experienced chef, or anyone who just enjoys great tasting food. Once one becomes familiar with the wonderful ingredients available in the vast world of vegetarian cuisine, creating meals becomes a delight. Each dish prepared a few times from any of the wonderful recipes presented by Chef Star soon becomes easy-to-prepare favorites.

Food to Heal the Planet

Not only does the diner's health and taste buds benefit from the many treasures awaiting in Chef Star's recipes, our precious but endangered planet gains as well. You see, to create the tremendous amounts of meats and dairy products required to satisfy our national craving for animal products, tremendous damage is inflicted upon our environment. Staggering amounts of forests are cleared, top soil is eroded and rivers and drinking wells are polluted by manure and agri-chemicals, all in the name of "cheap" cheeseburgers and T-bone steaks. We are squandering our children's ability to grow their food in the future, just to satisfy our meat addiction.

Again, the timely and appropriate recipes and philosophy presented in Chef Star's pure and healthy vegetarian cookbook are also allies of Mother Earth. An evolution in our personal and national diets toward more plant-based foods will allow our troubled ecosystem to heal, as less meat production would mean less top soil erosion, water pollution and, of course, less animal suffering.

So if you are exploring vegetarian cuisine to improve your health, to help heal the planet, to be gentler with our fellow creatures or just to enjoy great food, you are holding the right book in your hands. Explore, expand, but most of all, enjoy. You're in good hands with Chef Star. Bon appetit!

Michael Klaper, M.D.
Maui, Hawaii

Glossary

Agar-Agar Marine algae based thickener

Arrowroot powder A starch made from arrowroot plant

Carob Flavoring made from evergreen tree pods

Kaffree Roma® A coffee substitute, made from roasted malt barley, barley and chicory

Kelp Seaweed

Mirin Liquid from cultured rice and spring water

Miso Thick fermented paste of cooked soybeans, rice and salt

Nori/Ginger Spice Seaweed mixture seasoning

Nutritional Yeast A molasses-based cheesy flavored source of B-vitamins

Tahini Crushed sesame seeds

Tamari Organic whole soybean sauce

Turmeric Powdered rootstalk of a plant of India

Tempeh Partially cooked fermented soybeans

Tofu Soybean curd

Soymage® A replacement dairy cheese

Soy Mayonnaise Mayonnaise made with soy beans—contains no eggs

Sorghum Syrup made from certain grasses-used as a sweetener

Spike® All-purpose seasoning with 39 herbs

Vege Sal® All-purpose seasoning that is very low in sodium

BREAKFASTS

Star's Tofu Omelet

1/2 ONION, diced	3 Tbsp. NUTRITIONAL
1/2 GREEN PEPPER, diced	YEAST
3 MUSHROOM CAPS, sliced	1 Tbsp. TAMARI
2 Tbsp. VEGETABLE OIL	1/4 tsp. TURMERIC
1 (8 oz.) TOFU CAKE	1/2 tsp. VEGE SAL®

Sauté onion, green pepper and mushrooms in 1 tablespoon oil in omelet pan, remove from pan and set aside. Mix remaining ingredients in a bowl, mashing tofu into small pieces. Press 1/2 of mixture in omelet pan, fill sautéed vegetables into the middle and cover with remaining tofu mixture. Cook over medium heat until light brown, turn and lightly brown other side. Can also be baked at 350 degrees for 30 minutes in baking dish. Serves 2.

Per cup: Calories 278 (61% from fat), Protein 12.3g, Carb. 16.3g, Total Fat 19.8g, Sodium 808mg, Dietary Fiber 2.1g

Gelatin a la Hawaiian

1/2 cup WATER
2 tsp. AGAR-AGAR
1 cup PINEAPPLE
1 cup fresh STRAWBERRIES
1 cup COCONUT JUICE
3 Tbsp. SORGHUM
2 Tbsp. COCONUT MEAL

Place 1/2 cup water in small saucepan, add agar-agar, stir and bring to a boil. Pour agar-agar in blender, add remaining ingredients, except coconut meal. Blend and pour into sherbet glasses, chill. Before serving, sprinkle with coconut meal and garnish with berries.

Serves 3.

Per cup: Calories 192 (21% from fat), Protein 2.43g, Carb. 59g, Total Fat 7.1g, Sodium 91mg, Dietary Fiber 2.07g

Bran Breakfast

1/2 cup UNPROCESSED BRAN
3 Tbsp. RAW WHEAT GERM
4 Tbsp. hulled SUNFLOWER SEEDS
4 tsp. RAISINS
1/2 cup SOY MILK
CINNAMON

Mix the first four ingredients well. Cover with soy milk and sprinkle with cinnamon to taste.

Serves 1.

Per cup: Calories 684 (44% from fat), Protein 34g, Carb. 68g, Total Fat 35g, Sodium 22mg, Dietary Fiber 7.5g

Uncooked Applesauce

4 dried APRICOTS
4 APPLES
1/4 cup APPLE JUICE
1/2 cup SORGHUM

Cover apricots with water and soak until soft. Drain. Add all ingredients into a blender, blend until smooth. Chill and serve.

Serves 3.

Per cup: Calories 287 (2% from fat), Protein 0.82g, Carb. 75g, Total Fat 0.76g, Sodium 2.9mg, Dietary Fiber 4.6g

Dried Fruit Pizazz

1/2 cup FIGS
1/2 cup RAISINS
1/2 cup PRUNES
3 LEMON PEELS
1/4 cup dried APPLES

Cover fruit with water and simmer 1 hour.

Mix in:
1 Tbsp. SORGHUM
Sprinkle with:
1 Tbsp. chopped CASHEWS
2 ozs. PINE NUTS
1 Tbsp. chopped WALNUTS

Chill and serve.

Serves 2.

Per cup: Calories 494 (31% from fat), Protein 11.3g, Carb. 85g, Total Fat 19g, Sodium 44mg, Dietary Fiber 9.8g

Basic Tofu Yogurt

2 frozen BANANAS
1/4 cup APPLE JUICE
1 (8 oz.) TOFU CAKE
1 tsp. RICE SYRUP

Add all ingredients to a blender or food processor and blend until smooth and creamy. Chill and serve.

Variations:
- Add any fresh fruit you desire.
- Add walnuts, raisins.
- Add 1/4 teaspoon fresh mint.

Serves 2.

Per cup: Calories 222 (25% from fat), Protein 11.4g, Carb. 32.6g, Total Fat 6.5g, Sodium 10.9mg, Dietary Fiber 3.16g

Soy Banana Milk

3/4 cup SOY MILK   **1/4 tsp. SORGHUM**
1/2 frozen BANANA   **1 tsp. VANILLA**
1 BANANA

Add all ingredients to blender and blend until smooth. Great over cereal.

Serves 2.

Per cup: Calories 116 (16% from fat), Protein 3.4g, Carb. 22.4g, Total Fat 2.17g, Sodium 16.5mg, Dietary Fiber 3.2g

Fruit & Seed Mix

1/4 cup RAISINS
1/4 cup pitted PRUNES
1/4 cup hulled SUNFLOWER SEEDS
1/4 cup SESAME SEEDS
1 BANANA, sliced
1 tsp. BROWN RICE SYRUP
1/2 cup GRANOLA

Place raisins and prunes in a bowl, cover with water and soak overnight. Pour off water and add remaining ingredients. Chill and serve. Serves 3.

Per serving: Calories 463 (43% from fat), Protein 13.2g, Carb. 56g, Total Fat 23g, Sodium 21.6mg, Dietary Fiber 5g

Tofu Salsa Burrito

1 (12 oz.) TOFU CAKE, mashed
1 Tbsp. VEGETABLE OIL
3 Tbsp. NUTRITIONAL YEAST
1/4 tsp. SEA SALT
1/4 tsp. KELP
1/8 tsp. TURMERIC

Add all ingredients into a skillet and sauté over medium heat for about 8-10 minutes until lightly browned. Spoon mixture into 2 corn tortillas and top with 1 tablespoon salsa. Serves 2.

Per serving: Calories 267 (55% from fat), Protein 16.4g, Carb. 14.7g, Total Fat 16.7g, Sodium 532mg, Dietary Fiber 1.95g

Tofu Fruit Cream Cheese

1 (8 oz.) TOFU CAKE
1/8 tsp. SEA SALT
1/8 tsp. CARAWAY SEEDS
1 Tbsp. SOY MILK
1/8 cup PINEAPPLE
1/8 tsp. DILL WEED

Blend all ingredients in a blender until smooth. Chill and serve on bread, waffles, bagels, etc.

Serves 2.

Per 1/2 cup: Calories 105 (47% from fat), Protein 10.5g, Carb. 4.7g, Total Fat 6.1g, Sodium 151mg, Dietary Fiber 0.33g

Strawberry Spread

2 cups STRAWBERRIES
1/4 cup WATER
2 Tbsp. BERRY JUICE
1/4 cup BROWN RICE SYRUP
1 1/2 tsp. ARROWROOT POWDER

Cook strawberries in pot with water on low heat for 20 minutes. Add remaining ingredients, stirring continuously. Simmer for 20 more minutes. Chill and serve.

Serves 2.

Per cup: Calories 169 (4% from fat), Protein 0.98g, Carb. 32g, Total Fat 0.6g, Sodium 4.04mg, Dietary Fiber 3g

Cold Fruit Soup

2 PLUMS
1 PEAR
2 PEACHES

1/2 cup BLUEBERRIES
1/2 cup RAISINS
1 APPLE

Peel, pit and prepare fruit into bite-sized pieces and mix together in serving bowl.

Blend in blender until smooth:
1/2 cup APPLE JUICE
1 Tbsp. RICE SYRUP
1 frozen BANANA

Pour over fruit and top with:
1 Tbsp. CASHEW pieces

Serves 2.

Per cup: Calories 425 (8% from fat), Protein 4.3g, Carb. 97g, Total Fat 3.74g, Sodium 37mg, Dietary Fiber 13g

Hot Cereal of Grains

3 cups WATER
1/2 cup RYE FLAKES
1/2 cup WHEAT FLAKES
1/8 tsp. SEA SALT
1/8 tsp. VANILLA
1/8 tsp. CINNAMON
1 Tbsp. RICE SYRUP
1 tsp. MARGARINE

Mix grains, sea salt and water in saucepan. Cover and cook on medium heat for 8 minutes. Uncover and simmer for 30 minutes, stirring every 5 minutes. Add remaining ingredients, stir well and serve.

Serves 2-3.

Per cup: Calories 445 (8% from fat), Protein 15g, Carb. 84g, Total Fat 3.9g, Sodium 179mg, Dietary Fiber 14.3g

Pancakes of Buckwheat

Mix together dry ingredients:

1 1/2 cups BUCKWHEAT FLOUR
1/2 cup WHOLE WHEAT FLOUR
2 Tbsp. BAKING POWDER
1/2 tsp. SEA SALT
1/2 tsp. NUTMEG

Mix together liquid ingredients:

1 cup SOY MILK
1 cup FRUIT JUICE
1 Tbsp. VEGETABLE OIL

Mix together dry and liquid ingredients until smooth. Heat lightly oiled skillet over medium heat. Pour 1/4 - 1/2 cup batter to form each pancake. Flip over when top is bubbly and bottom is lightly browned. Serve with your favorite fruit syrup or soy margarine. Serves 3.

Per serving (2 pcs.-4" diam.): Calories 352 (9% from fat), Protein 11.2g, Carb. 160g, Total Fat 7.8g, Sodium 1247mg, Dietary Fiber 6g

Cherry Fruit Dip

1 cup TOFU YOGURT (see page 14)
1/2 cup CHERRY NATURAL CONSERVES
1/4 tsp. LEMON JUICE

Mix all ingredients together in a bowl. Chill and dip in your favorite cut fruit. Delicious!

Serves 2.

Per cup: Calories 279 (9% from fat), Protein 5.7g, Carb. 64g, Total Fat 3.25g, Sodium 5.6mg, Dietary Fiber 1.58g

Pancakes of Whole Wheat

3 cups WHOLE WHEAT FLOUR
2 Tbsp. BAKING POWDER
1 cup SOY MILK
1 Tbsp. VEGETABLE OIL
1 cup FRUIT JUICE (your choice)

Mix dry ingredients into bowl, add liquids and blend until smooth. Heat lightly oiled skillet over medium heat. Pour 1/4 - 1/2 cup batter to form each pancake. Flip over when top is bubbly and bottom is lightly browned. Serve with your favorite fruit syrup or soy margarine.

Serves 3.

Per serving (2 pcs.-4" diam.): Calories 517 (8% from fat), Protein 18.6g, Carb. 194g, Total Fat 8g, Sodium 874mg, Dietary Fiber 14g

Banana Surprise

Add in bowl:
2 ripe BANANAS,
    sliced 1/4 inch
1 cup BLACKBERRIES

Mix in:
1 tsp. BROWN RICE SYRUP

Top with:
3 Tbsp. CASHEW pieces

Serves 3.

Per cup: Calories 150 (26% from fat), Protein 2.43g, Carb. 27g, Total Fat 4.5g, Sodium 55mg, Dietary Fiber 4.3g

French Banana Toast

1 ripe BANANA
1 (8 oz.) TOFU CAKE
1 tsp. VEGETABLE OIL
3/4 cup SOY MILK
1/2 tsp. VANILLA
1 tsp. CINNAMON

Mix together all ingredients until smooth. Dip slices of whole wheat bread into batter, turning to coat both sides. Brown both sides in hot, lightly oiled skillet.

Serves 3.

Per slice: Calories 264 (29% from fat), Protein 13g, Carb. 36g, Total Fat 8.8g, Sodium 292mg, Dietary Fiber 6.1g

Sweet Fruit Salad

Add in bowl:
1/2 cup fresh STRAWBERRIES
1/2 cup fresh RASPBERRIES
1/2 cup fresh BLUEBERRIES
1 NECTARINE, sliced

Mix in:
2 Tbsp. PINEAPPLE JUICE
1 Tbsp. BROWN RICE SYRUP

Sprinkle with:
CASHEW NUTS, finely chopped

Chill and serve.

Serves 3.

Per cup: Calories 143 (38% from fat), Protein 2.7g, Carb. 18.4g, Total Fat 5.8g, Sodium 74mg, Dietary Fiber 5.4g

SOUPS
&
SANDWICHES

Winter Soup

1 cup ONIONS, diced
2 ZUCCHINI, cubed
2 cups VEGETABLE STOCK
1 bunch SPINACH
2 tsp. SOY MARGARINE

1 1/2 Tbsp. BASIL
1 Tbsp. LEMON JUICE
Dash SEA SALT
Dash PEPPER

Sauté onions and zucchini in soy margarine in a soup pot until onions are soft and transparent. Add stock and bring to a boil. Add spinach, salt and pepper, cover pot and cook 5 minutes. Pureé in blender, return to pot and simmer 5 minutes. Add lemon juice. Serves 3-4.

Per cup: Calories 66 (32% from fat), Protein 3.3g, Carb. 9.8g, Total Fat 2.7g, Sodium 72mg, Dietary Fiber 4.8g

Cabbage Soup

2 ONIONS
2 CARROTS
2 GARLIC CLOVES
1 head CABBAGE
1 tsp. VEGETABLE OIL
2 Tbsp. TAMARI
2 cups TOMATO JUICE

6 cups VEGETABLE
    STOCK
1 tsp. PARSLEY
1/2 tsp. BASIL
1/4 cup APPLE JUICE
1/8 tsp. CAYENNE

Dice onions and carrots. In a large saucepan sauté onions, carrots, crushed garlic and shredded cabbage in vegetable oil and tamari until carrots are soft. Add remaining ingredients and simmer for 55 minutes.

Serves 6-8.

Per cup: Calories 86 (11% from fat), Protein 3.65g, Carb. 18g, Total Fat 1.24g, Sodium 477mg, Dietary Fiber 2.6g

Tomato-Onion Soup

3/4 cup ONIONS, chopped
3/4 cup VEGETABLE STOCK or WATER
2 cups pureed fresh TOMATOES
1 tsp. SWEET BASIL
2 med. GARLIC CLOVES, pressed
1/4 tsp. PEPPER
1 (8 oz.) TOFU CAKE

Add all ingredients, except tofu, to a medium saucepan. Bring to a boil, cover, simmer 15-20 minutes. Blend tofu in blender until smooth and stir into mixture, simmer for 5 minutes.

Serves 3.

Per cup: Calories 150 (22% from fat), Protein 10.3g, Carb. 22.7g, Total Fat 4.2g, Sodium 46mg, Dietary Fiber 0.72g

Seaweed Miso Soup

ALARIA SEAWEED, 24-inch piece
2 med. ONIONS, sliced
2 tsp. SESAME OIL
6 cups WATER
1 1/2 tsp. RED MISO
3/4 cup SCALLIONS

Soak seaweed in water until it softens, then chop. Sauté onions in oil in medium saucepan until transparent, add seaweed and sauté until greenish. Add water, simmer 30 minutes. Mix miso and 1/2 cup water in a cup and add to soup. Simmer 3 minutes, sprinkle chopped scallions on top before serving.

Serves 4-6.

Per cup: Calories 41 (33% from fat), Protein 3.1g, Carb. 6.2g, Total Fat 2.07g, Sodium 104mg, Dietary Fiber 1.25g

Mushroom Soup

3 cups VEGETABLE
    STOCK
2 CELERY STALKS
1 med. ONION
8 oz. MUSHROOMS
1 Tbsp. SOY
    MARGARINE
1 tsp. BASIL
2 Tbsp. TAMARI
1 tsp. MISO

Bring vegetable stock to boil, add diced celery and onions. Simmer for 10 minutes. Slice and sauté mushrooms in soy margarine for 5 minutes and add with spices to stock, simmer 15 minutes. Mix miso with small amount of water until dissolved and add to soup just before serving.

Serves 4.

Per cup: Calories 48 (46% from fat), Protein 3.6g, Carb. 4.9g, Total Fat 3.16g, Sodium 609mg, Dietary Fiber 1.18g

Vegetable Corn Soup

Blend in blender until smooth:
1 cup WHOLE KERNEL CORN
1/2 cup SOY MILK
1 Tbsp. SOY MARGARINE

Cook in saucepan over medium heat for 5 minutes:
1/2 cup WATER
1/2 cup CARROTS, diced
3/4 cup ONIONS, diced

Add to saucepan:
blended corn mixture
1/2 cup ZUCCHINI, diced
1 cup LIMA BEANS, cooked
1 tsp. BASIL
1/2 tsp. THYME
2 Tbsp. TAMARI

Simmer for 10 minutes and serve.

Serves 3-4.

Per cup: Calories 145 (22% from fat), Protein 7.6g, Carb. 23.7g, Total Fat 4g, Sodium 703mg, Dietary Fiber 6.6g

Onion Bean Soup

1 cup mixed PINTO and KIDNEY BEANS
1 cup ONIONS, diced
1 GARLIC CLOVE, minced
1 tsp. VEGE SAL®
1/2 tsp. SEA SALT
1 Tbsp. TAMARI
1 qt. WATER

Cover beans with water and soak overnight. Pour off soaking water and rinse beans. Add beans and onions to water, bring to a boil. Add remaining ingredients, simmer for 1 hour 10 minutes.

Serves 2.

Per cup: Calories 138 (4% from fat), Protein 8.4g, Carb. 26.4g, Total Fat 0.58g, Sodium 2053mg, Dietary Fiber 10.3g

Miso Soup

1 head CABBAGE
2 Tbsp. VEGETABLE OIL
3 CARROTS
2 CELERY STALKS
1 cup VEGETABLE STOCK
1/2 tsp. SEA SALT
1/8 tsp. CAYENNE
1 (8 oz.) TOFU CAKE
1 1/2 Tbsp. MISO

Sauté shredded cabbage, diced carrots and diced onions in saucepan until soft. Add stock and spices, simmer for 25 minutes. Add cubed tofu, simmer 10 minutes. Dissolve miso in 1/2 cup water and add before serving.

Serves 2-4.

Per cup: Calories 268 (38% from fat), Protein 22g, Carb. 32g, Total Fat 14.8g, Sodium 827mg, Dietary Fiber 4.7g

Vegetable Soup Supreme

1 ONION
1/2 cup GREEN BEANS
2 CARROTS
2 YELLOW CROOKNECK SQUASH
4 TOMATOES
1 Tbsp. PARSLEY
1 Tbsp. NUTRITIONAL YEAST
1 POTATO
1 cup EGGPLANT
2 CELERY STALKS
2 BOK CHOY STALKS
1/2 cup MUSHROOMS
1 Tbsp. VEGETABLE OIL
8 cups VEGETABLE STOCK
1 tsp. BASIL
1 tsp. SEA SALT

Dice all vegetables and lightly sauté in saucepan in vegetable oil until soft. Add vegetable stock and seasonings. Simmer for 50 minutes.

Serves 6-8.

Per cup: Calories 78 (26% from fat), Protein 2.3g, Carb. 13g, Total Fat 2.4g, Sodium 411mg, Dietary Fiber 2.5g

Vegetable Peanut Butter Soup

3 CELERY STALKS
2 CARROTS
1 ONION
1 Tbsp. VEGETABLE OIL
1 Tbsp. WHOLE WHEAT FLOUR
4 qts. VEGETABLE STOCK
3 TOMATOES, peeled
1/2 med. CABBAGE
1/8 tsp. CAYENNE PEPPER
1 tsp. SEA SALT
1 Tbsp. OREGANO
1 cup CHUNKY PEANUT BUTTER

Dice all hard vegetables and sauté in large pot in vegetable oil until soft. Add flour and mix well. Add vegetable stock and bring to a boil. Purée tomatoes and cabbage in blender and add to soup with spices. Stir in peanut butter and simmer for about 20 minutes.

Serves 6-8.

Per cup: Calories 287 (60% from fat), Protein 11.3g, Carb. 19.7g, Total Fat 20.8g, Sodium 389mg, Dietary Fiber 4.4g

Tofu Cream Soup

1 med. ONION
1 CARROT
4 CELERY STALKS
1 Tbsp. VEGETABLE OIL
1 1/2 tsp. VEGETABLE OIL
2 cups WATER

2 cups SOY MILK
1 (8 oz.) TOFU CAKE
1 tsp. CELERY SEED
1/8 tsp. CAYENNE
3 POTATOES

Dice onions, carrots and celery and sauté in saucepan in vegetable oil until tender. Add water, soy milk, mashed tofu and spices. Bring to a boil and add cubed potatoes. Simmer until potatoes are soft.

Serves 3-4.

Per cup: Calories 119 (36% from fat), Protein 6.3g, Carb. 13.8g, Total Fat 5.1g, Sodium 41.6mg, Dietary Fiber 1.6g

Barley Medley

4 qts. WATER
1 cup WHOLE BARLEY
7 CARROTS
4 CELERY STALKS
1 1/2 lbs. GREEN BEANS
1 lb. TOMATOES
2 ONIONS

1 1/2 Tbsp. VEGE-
    TABLE OIL
2 Tbsp. TAMARI
1 tsp. THYME
1 Tbsp. PARSLEY
1 tsp. VEGE SAL®

Cook barley in water until soft, dice all vegetables and add to barley. Add oil, tamari and spices, leaving parsley until just before serving.

Serves 6.

Per cup: Calories 236 (16% from fat), Protein 8.3g, Carb. 45g, Total Fat 4.6g, Sodium 616mg, Dietary Fiber 6.5g

Lentil Soup

1 lb. LENTILS
3 qts. WATER
3 CELERY STALKS
3 sm. ONIONS
3 med. CARROTS
1/4 tsp. CHILI PEPPER

1 Tbsp. PARSLEY
1/2 GREEN PEPPER
2 GARLIC CLOVES
3 TOMATOES
2 Tbsp. OLIVE OIL

Bring lentils and water to a boil in a saucepan and then simmer for 45 minutes. Add diced hard vegetables, blended tomatoes and spices. Simmer until all vegetables are soft.

Serves 4-5.

Per cup: Calories 246 (26% from fat), Protein 12.7g, Carb. 40g, Total Fat 8.1g, Sodium 93mg, Dietary Fiber 6.7g

Squash Soup

1 oz. DRY KELP
1 1/2 lg. ONIONS
6 cups WINTER SQUASH
3/4 cup PARSLEY
2 Tbsp. TAMARI

Cover kelp with water and simmer 10 minutes. Add onion and squash and cover with water. Simmer till squash is soft, add chopped parsley and tamari. Blend in blender.

Serves 3-5.

Per cup: Calories 181 (9% from fat), Protein 6.7g, Carb. 41g, Total Fat 1.97g, Sodium 565mg, Dietary Fiber 9.7g

Broccoli Cream Soup

1/2 ONION
1 Tbsp. SOY MARGARINE
1 1/2 cups BROCCOLI
1/8 cup WHOLE WHEAT FLOUR
3 cups VEGETABLE STOCK
1 cup SOY MILK
1 tsp. NUTRITIONAL YEAST
1 tsp. SEA SALT
dash BLACK PEPPER

Sauté diced onion and chopped broccoli in margarine in saucepan. Stir in whole wheat flour and cook over medium heat for 7 minutes. Add vegetable stock and bring to a boil stirring frequently. Lower heat and simmer for 25 minutes. Add remaining ingredients, stir and serve.

Serves 4.

Per cup: Calories 71 (49% from fat), Protein 3.3g, Carb. 6.5g, Total Fat 4.2g, Sodium 615mg, Dietary Fiber 1.62g

Soup de Bok Choy

2 qts. VEGETABLE STOCK   **2 tsp. SEA SALT**
1 (12 oz.) TOFU CAKE   **1 bunch BOK CHOY**
1 med. ONION   **1 tsp. RED MISO**

Bring vegetable stock to a boil, cube tofu, chop onion and add to stock along with salt. Simmer for 15 minutes. Chop bok choy into bite-sized pieces, add and simmer for 4 minutes. Dilute miso in small amount of water and add before serving.

Serves 6-8.

Per cup: Calories 50 (40% from fat), Protein 6g, Carb. 3.14g, Total Fat 2.7g, Sodium 707mg, Dietary Fiber 0.66g

Tomato Sprout Sandwich

2 slices WHOLE WHEAT BREAD
2 Tbsp. SOY MAYONNAISE
1/2 TOMATO, sliced
1/2 AVOCADO, sliced
2 slices ONION
2 LETTUCE LEAVES
ALFALFA SPROUTS

Cover one slice of bread with soy mayonnaise and stack remaining ingredients. Top with second slice of bread.

*Note: Many of the casserole and burger recipes in the Main Dish chapter can be used the following day for delicious sandwiches.

Per sandwich: Calories 515 (66% from fat), Protein 8.7g, Carb. 37g, Total Fat 39.5g, Sodium 454mg, Dietary Fiber 9.3g

Tempeh Sloppy Joe's

4 oz. TEMPEH
1 Tbsp. VEGETABLE OIL
1 WHOLE WHEAT BUN
TOMATO, sliced thin
ONION, sliced thin
1 Tbsp. MUSTARD

Crumble tempeh and sauté in vegetable oil until brown. Fill bun with hot tempeh and add remaining ingredients. Add sprouts if you desire.

Per sandwich: Calories 489 (41% from fat), Protein 23g, Carb. 53g, Total Fat 23g, Sodium 490mg, Dietary Fiber 10g

Broiled Tofu Sandwich

2 1-inch slices TOFU
1 cup TAMARI
2 slices TOMATO
2 thinly sliced pieces ONION
2 LETTUCE LEAVES
dash PEPPER
2 slices WHOLE WHEAT BREAD

Marinate tofu slices in tamari for 15 minutes. Broil tofu on both sides until slightly browned. Layer all ingredients between bread slices. Other garnishes could be ketchup, mustard or soy mayonnaise.

Per sandwich: Calories 371 (15% from fat), Protein 40g, Carb. 45g, Total Fat 6.7g, Sodium 1636mg, Dietary Fiber 6.5g

Peanut Butter & Jam Supreme

2 slices WHOLE WHEAT BREAD
1 Tbsp. CHUNKY PEANUT BUTTER
1 Tbsp. FRUIT JAM
1/2 BANANA, halved
1 Tbsp. RAISINS
1 Tbsp. WALNUTS, chopped

Layer all ingredients between slices of bread.

Per sandwich: Calories 408 (31% from fat), Protein 10.8g, Carb. 63g, Total Fat 14.7g, Sodium 283mg, Dietary Fiber 8.5g

SALADS
&
DRESSINGS

Mushroom Spinach Salad

2 GARLIC CLOVES, mashed
1 head ROMAINE LETTUCE
1/2 head BUTTER LETTUCE
1/4 head RED CABBAGE, shredded
2 GREEN PEPPERS, sliced
1 med. RED ONION, sliced thin
1 lb. FRESH SPINACH, chopped
1/2 lb. MUSHROOMS, sliced

Rub mashed garlic into sides of a wooden bowl. Tear lettuce into bite-sized pieces, add all ingredients into the bowl and toss well. Chill 3 hours, garnish with tomatoes and serve with your favorite oil and vinegar dressing.

Serves 4-6.

Per serving: Calories 250 (6% from fat), Protein 14.8g, Carb. 51g, Total Fat 1.73g, Sodium 275mg, Dietary Fiber 18g

Carrot Salad

1 lb. CARROTS, grated
1/4 head CABBAGE, shredded
2 Tbsp. RAISINS
1/2 ONION, diced
1/2 tsp. GARLIC POWDER

1/4 cup TAHINI
2 Tbsp. TAMARI
1 tsp. LEMON JUICE
1/8 tsp. SEA SALT
1/2 tsp. DILL WEED

Mix all ingredients into a salad bowl and stir until all ingredients are moist. Chill and serve.

Serves 3-4.

Per serving: Calories 179 (40% from fat), Protein 5.8g, Carb. 23.7g, Total Fat 8.6g, Sodium 645mg, Dietary Fiber 2.25g

Garden Salad

1/2 head RED LETTUCE
1/2 head BUTTER LETTUCE
1/4 head ROMAINE LETTUCE
1 med. ZUCCHINI, diced
1 leaf KALE, chopped
2 GARLIC CLOVES, finely minced
1 cup ALFALFA SPROUTS
1 leaf SWISS CHARD, chopped
1 cup SPINACH, chopped
1 AVOCADO, peeled and sliced
1 RED ONION, sliced thin

Tear all lettuce into bite-sized pieces and mix all ingredients in a salad bowl. Toss well and add your favorite dressing.

Serves 4-6.

Per serving: Calories 101 (51% from fat), Protein 4g, Carb. 10g, Total Fat 6.5g, Sodium 45mg, Dietary Fiber 3.7g

Pepper Bean Salad

1 1/2 cups cooked PINTO BEANS
1 CELERY STALK, chopped
1 med. ONION, diced
1 cup mixed GREEN and RED PEPPERS, diced
1 tsp. SEA SALT
1/2 tsp. OREGANO
1/2 tsp. THYME
1 tsp. BASIL

Mix all ingredients together in a salad bowl. Serve with oil and vinegar dressing or your favorite dressing.

Serves 3-4.

Per serving: Calories 140 (4% from fat), Protein 7.9g, Carb. 27g, Total Fat 0.65g, Sodium 769mg, Dietary Fiber 4.6g

Zucchini Salad

3 CARROTS
6 ZUCCHINI
1/2 ONION
1/2 GREEN PEPPER
1 GARLIC CLOVE
1/2 tsp. THYME
1/2 tsp. CHERVIL
dash PEPPER
1/2 cup WATER
2 Tbsp. VINEGAR
1/2 tsp. BASIL
1/8 tsp. DRY MUSTARD

Shred carrots, zucchini and onion. Dice green pepper, mince garlic and toss together in salad bowl. Put remaining ingredients in blender and blend for a few seconds. Add dressing to vegetables and chill for 2 hours. Garnish with tomato wedges and serve.

Serves 4-6.

Per serving: Calories 55 (7% from fat), Protein 2.77g, Carb. 12g, Total Fat 0.46g, Sodium 24mg, Dietary Fiber 5.8g

Cole Slaw

1 head RED CABBAGE, shredded
2 CARROTS, shredded
4 GREEN ONIONS, chopped
1 tsp. CELERY SEED
3/4 cup SOY MAYONNAISE
1/8 cup RICE VINEGAR
1/4 cup RICE SYRUP
1 Tbsp. DIJON MUSTARD

Place all shredded and chopped vegetables in a salad bowl. Mix together remaining ingredients in small bowl to make dressing. Pour dressing over vegetables and toss well. Garnish with tomato wedges. Serves 4-6.

Per cup: Calories 318 (85% from fat), Protein 2.06g, Carb. 8.4g, Total Fat 27g, Sodium 242mg, Dietary Fiber 3.9g

Avocado Delight

2 AVOCADOS
1 CELERY STALK
1/4 GREEN PEPPER
2 TOMATO slices
1 Tbsp. SOY MAYONNAISE
1 Tbsp. ground WALNUTS
2 BLACK OLIVES
1 tsp. TAMARI

Scoop out center of avocados and mash in a bowl. Finely chop celery, green pepper, tomato and olives and mix all ingredients except black olives together. Fill avocado shells with the mixture and garnish with olives. Serves 2-4.

Per serving: Calories 272 (81% from fat), Protein 3.6g, Carb. 10g, Total Fat 26.6g, Sodium 214mg, Dietary Fiber 3.1g

Leaf-Sprout Salad

1/2 head BUTTER LETTUCE
1/2 head ROMAINE LETTUCE
4 MUSHROOMS, thinly sliced
1/2 RED ONION, thinly sliced
1 cup ALFALFA SPROUTS
1/2 cup BEAN SPROUTS
1 cup SUNFLOWER SPROUTS
2 Tbsp. RAISINS
2 Tbsp. SUNFLOWER SEEDS

Tear lettuce into bite-sized pieces and toss all ingredients in a large salad bowl. Squeeze lemon juice over salad to taste and serve with your favorite dressing.

Serves 3-4.

Per serving: Calories 187 (49% from fat), Protein 10g, Carb. 16.7g, Total Fat 11.3g, Sodium 15.5mg, Dietary Fiber 3.8g

Greek Olive Salad

1 (8 oz.) TOFU CAKE
2 TOMATOES
1/2 cup GREEK OLIVES
1/2 RED ONION
2 CUCUMBERS

Cut tofu and tomatoes into 3/4-inch cubes, slice cucumber and red onion very thin. Mix all ingredients in salad bowl and serve with your favorite Italian dressing.

Serves 3-4.

Per serving: Calories 158 (47% from fat), Protein 9.2g, Carb. 13.6g, Total Fat 9.1g, Sodium 457mg, Dietary Fiber 3.05g

Potpourri Special Salad

1/2 head ROMAINE LETTUCE
1 cup FRESH SPINACH
1/2 RED BELL PEPPER, diced
1/2 RED ONION, sliced thin
1 AVOCADO, cubed
2 ENDIVE leaves
1/2 CUCUMBER, sliced
1 TOMATO, diced
1 Tbsp. NUTRITIONAL YEAST
1 Tbsp. RAISINS

Tear lettuce and spinach into bite-sized pieces and toss together with other ingredients in a large salad bowl. Serve with your favorite salad dressing.

Serves 3-4.

Per serving: Calories 161 (53% from fat), Protein 5g, Carb. 16g, Total Fat 10.6g, Sodium 61mg, Dietary Fiber 4.8g

Beet Salad

3 cups raw BEETS
1 CARROT
3 Tbsp. OLIVE OIL
4 Tbsp. VINEGAR

2 Tbsp. PARSLEY
3 lg. ROMAINE LEAVES
1/2 CUCUMBER
3 RADISHES

Grate beets and carrot, add oil, vinegar and parsley. Line plate with lettuce leaves, put beet mixture on leaves and garnish with thinly sliced cucumber and radishes.

Serves 3-4.

Per cup: Calories 203 (62% from fat), Protein 2.74g, Carb. 17.3g, Total Fat 14.2g, Sodium 96mg, Dietary Fiber 2.1g

Potato Salad

5 POTATOES, cooked,
   peeled and cubed
1 1/2 GREEN PEPPERS,
   chopped
2 CARROTS, shredded
1 CELERY STALK, diced
4 GREEN ONIONS, diced
1 cup SOY MAYONNAISE

2 Tbsp. TAMARI
1 tsp. BASIL
1 tsp. PAPRIKA
1 tsp. GARLIC POWDER
1 tsp. OREGANO
dash RED PEPPER
dash SEA SALT

Add potatoes and other vegetables to a large bowl. Combine soy mayonnaise and spices to make dressing and gently fold dressing into vegetables. Chill and serve.

Serves 4-6.

Per cup: Calories 461 (68% from fat), Protein 4.6g, Carb. 34g, Total Fat 36g, Sodium 682mg, Dietary Fiber 1.32g

Cucumber Salad

1 cup SPINACH
3 cups CUCUMBERS
1/2 cup RED ONION
1/4 cup fresh PARSLEY
2 CELERY STALKS
2 cups TOMATOES
dash SEA SALT

Chop spinach and parsley, dice tomatoes, celery and onion. Peel and slice very thin cucumber. Toss all ingredients together in salad bowl. Serve with your favorite dressing.

Serves 4-6.

Per serving: Calories 33.6 (8% from fat), Protein 2.2g, Carb. 7g, Total Fat 0.35g, Sodium 50mg, Dietary Fiber 2.5g

Tabouli Salad

1/2 cup BULGUR WHEAT
3/4 cup VEGETABLE STOCK
1/4 cup diced ONIONS
1 tsp. fresh MINT
1/4 cup fresh PARSLEY
dash GARLIC POWDER
1/2 TOMATO
3 RADISHES
1 Tbsp. LEMON JUICE
1 1/2 Tbsp. VEGETABLE OIL
dash CAYENNE
dash ONION POWDER

Soak bulgur in water for 5 hours, strain and squeeze out excess water. Dice onion. Peel and chop tomato, chop radishes and mince mint and parsley. Mix all ingredients together until well blended.

Serves 3-4.

Per serving: Calories 153 (40% from fat), Protein 3.4g, Carb. 20.6g, Total Fat 7.2g, Sodium 13.3mg, Dietary Fiber 4.65

Pasta Salad

1 package (12 oz.) MACARONI SPIRALS
4 GREEN ONIONS, chopped
2 TOMATOES, chopped
1 CUCUMBER, chopped
1 RED BELL PEPPER, chopped
1 cup SOY MAYONNAISE
1 Tbsp. SALAD MUSTARD
1 Tbsp. TAMARI
1/8 cup RICE VINEGAR
1/4 cup BROWN RICE VINEGAR
1 tsp. CELERY SEED
1 Tbsp. PARSLEY

Cook pasta and mix in a salad bowl with other vegetables. Combine other ingredients to create dressing and pour over pasta and vegetables. Stir well, chill and serve. Serves 6-8.

Per serving: Calories 386 (61% from fat), Protein 6.3g, Carb. 31.6g, Total Fat 26.6g, Sodium 357mg, Dietary Fiber 1.6g

Fruit Mold Salad

3 cups PAPAYA JUICE
1/4 cup AGAR-AGAR flakes
1 (8 oz.) TOFU CAKE, blended
2 Tbsp. ORGANIC RICE SYRUP
2 cups WALNUTS, chopped
1 cup CARROTS, shredded
1/2 cup RAISINS
1/2 tsp. VANILLA

Soak agar-agar flakes in juice for 10 minutes, simmer for 15 minutes. Mix all ingredients and pour into mold. Chill for 6 hours and serve. Serves 4-6.

Per serving: Calories 502 (44% from fat), Protein 18g, Carb. 72g, Total Fat 31g, Sodium 23.4mg, Dietary Fiber 3.8g

Orange-Onion Salad

1 lg. bunch SPINACH
6 ORANGES
1 VIDALIA ONION
4 Tbsp. WATER
2 Tbsp. APPLE JUICE

1 tsp. RICE VINEGAR
1 GARLIC CLOVE
1 tsp. SPIKE®
1/2 tsp. DRY MUSTARD

Tear spinach into bite-sized pieces. Peel oranges, remove all skin and cube. Toss spinach, orange cubes and chopped onion in a salad bowl. Blend remaining ingredients and pour over salad when ready to serve.

Serves 3-4.

Per serving: Calories 158 (4% from fat), Protein 4.9g, Carb. 37.6g, Total Fat 0.71g, Sodium 430mg, Dietary Fiber 8g

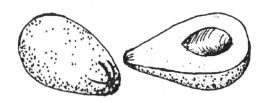

Avocado Salad Supreme

1/2 head ROMAINE LETTUCE
2 WHITE RADISHES
1 CUCUMBER

3 TOMATOES
2 AVOCADOS

Tear lettuce into bite-sized pieces and cover plate to form a bed of lettuce. Dice radishes, cucumber, tomatoes and cover center of lettuce bed. Slice avocados and arrange on outer edges of plate. Eat plain or use your favorite dressing.

Serves 2-4.

Per serving: Calories 253 (66% from fat), Protein 5g, Carb. 18.5g, Total Fat 20.6g, Sodium 34mg, Dietary Fiber 4.6g

Summer Melon Salad

1 cup WATERMELON
1 cup HONEYDEW
1 cup CANTALOUPE
1 Tbsp. crushed WALNUTS
2 Tbsp. COCONUT FLAKES
4 Tbsp. RAISINS

Cut all melon into bite-sized pieces and combine in salad bowl, garnish with walnuts, coconut flakes and raisins. Chill and serve.

Serves 2-4.

Per serving: Calories 177 (24% from fat), Protein 3.2g, Carb. 33g, Total Fat 5g, Sodium 47mg, Dietary Fiber 3.5g

Tropical Salad

1 MANGO
1/2 PAPAYA
1 BANANA
1/2 cup PINEAPPLE
2 Tbsp. COCONUT FLAKES

Slice mango, papaya and banana, dice pineapple. Combine together and garnish with coconut.

Serves 2-3.

Per serving: Calories 157 (19% from fat), Protein 1.48g, Carb. 33g, Total Fat 3.6g, Sodium 27.5mg, Dietary Fiber 3.3g

Avocado Dressing

1 cup ripe AVOCADO
1/2 cup WATER
1 LEMON

1 tsp. DIJON MUSTARD
2 tsp. SORGHUM

Combine all ingredients in blender and blend until smooth. Serves 2.

Per serving (3 tbsp.): Calories 181 (69% from fat), Protein 2.2g, Carb. 13.5g, Total Fat 15.2g, Sodium 44mg, Dietary Fiber 1.96g

Mustard Dressing

1/2 cup DIJON MUSTARD
1 cup APPLE CIDER
   VINEGAR

1 tsp. GARLIC POWDER
1 cup OLIVE OIL
1 Tbsp. LEMON JUICE

Blend all ingredients well in a blender. Serves 4-6.

Per serving (3 tbsp.): Calories 412 (87% from fat), Protein 1.07g, Carb. 14.8g, Total Fat 46g, Sodium 306mg, Dietary Fiber 0.15g

Vinaigrette Dressing

3/4 Tbsp. DIJON MUSTARD
6 Tbsp. SAFFLOWER OIL
1/2 tsp. LEMON JUICE
5 Tbsp. APPLE CIDER
   VINEGAR

1 Tbsp. WATER
1 tsp. PEPPER
dash SEA SALT

Blend all ingredients in a blender until smooth. Chill and serve. Serves 2-4.

Per serving (3 tbsp.): Calories 248 (89% from fat), Protein 0.22g, Carb. 7.4g, Total Fat 28g, Sodium 56mg, Dietary Fiber 0.02g

Lime & Lemon Dressing

2 Tbsp. WATER
4 Tbsp. OLIVE OIL
1/4 tsp. BLACK PEPPER
1 1/2 Tbsp. LIME JUICE

2 Tbsp. PARSLEY
1 tsp. VEGE SAL®
3 Tbsp. LEMON JUICE

Combine all ingredients in a blender and blend until smooth. Chill and serve. Serves 2-4.

Per serving (3 tbsp.): Calories 167 (95% from fat), Protein 0.17g, Carb. 1.97g, Total Fat 18.7g, Sodium 388mg, Dietary Fiber 0.10g

Herb Dressing

6 STRAWBERRIES
2 Tbsp. VEGETABLE OIL
4 Tbsp. THYME
2 Tbsp. TARRAGON
2 Tbsp. ROSEMARY
1 Tbsp. SEA SALT

1 tsp. BLACK PEPPER
1/2 tsp. CELERY SEED
1 tsp. CURRY POWDER
4 Tbsp. BASIL
1/2 tsp. LEMON JUICE

Combine all ingredients in blender and blend till smooth. Chill and serve. Serves 2-4.

Per serving (3 tbsp.): Calories 139 (60% from fat), Protein 2.6g, Carb. 13.2g, Total Fat 10.7g, Sodium 2265mg, Dietary Fiber 0.5g

Tofu Dressing

1 (8 oz.) TOFU CAKE
2 Tbsp. OLIVE OIL
1/4 tsp. CARAWAY SEEDS
1 Tbsp. PEANUT BUTTER
1/4 tsp. GARLIC POWDER
2 Tbsp. ONION POWDER

1 1/4 cup WATER
2 Tbsp. TAMARI
1/4 tsp. DILL WEED
1 GARLIC CLOVE
3 Tbsp. LEMON JUICE

Combine all ingredients in blender and blend until smooth. Chill and serve. Serves 4.

Per serving (3 tbsp.): Calories 151 (67% from fat), Protein 7.6g, Carb. 6g, Total Fat 12g, Sodium 532mg, Dietary Fiber 0.38g

Thousand Island Dressing

1 (8 oz.) TOFU CAKE
1/2 cup KETCHUP (no sugar)
1/4 tsp. SEA SALT
1/2 SWEET PICKLE
1 Tbsp. PARSLEY
2 Tbsp. VEGETABLE OIL
3/4 tsp. ONION POWDER
1 tsp. GARLIC POWDER
6 GREEN OLIVES

Combine all ingredients in blender and blend until smooth.

Serves 3-4.

Per serving (3 tbsp.): Calories 230 (55% from fat), Protein 8.2g, Carb. 19g, Total Fat 15g, Sodium 1018mg, Dietary Fiber 0.66g

Mixed Vegetable Dressing

1/2 AVOCADO, peeled
1 CELERY STALK
1 TOMATO, peeled
1/4 cup CHIVES
1/4 cup fresh PARSLEY
1/2 cup ONION
1 cup WATER
4 Tbsp. APPLE CIDER VINEGAR
2 tsp. VEGE SAL®

Combine all ingredients in a blender and blend till smooth. Chill and serve.

Serves 4-6.

Per serving (3 tbsp.): Calories 45 (46% from fat), Protein 0.89g, Carb. 7.3g, Total Fat 3.1g, Sodium 476mg, Dietary Fiber 1.12g

French Dressing

2 cups PEANUT OIL
3/4 cup CIDER VINEGAR
1 Tbsp. DIJON MUSTARD
1 Tbsp. TOMATO JUICE

1 Tbsp. SORGHUM
dash SEA SALT
dash PEPPER

Blend all ingredients in a blender until smooth. Chill and serve. Serves 4-6.

Per serving (3 tbsp.): Calories 818 (94% from fat), Protein 0.15g, Carb. 12.7g, Total Fat 90g, Sodium 50mg, Dietary Fiber 0.04g

Garden Dressing

1/3 cup BROCCOLI
1/3 cup CELERY
1/3 cup ZUCCHINI
2 cups WATER
5 Tbsp. TAMARI
2 COMFREY leaves
1 tsp. PARSLEY

5 Tbsp. PEANUT BUTTER
2 Tbsp. LEMON JUICE
1/2 ONION
2 GARLIC CLOVES
6 Tbsp. VEGETABLE OIL
1 tsp. BASIL

Combine all ingredients in a blender and blend until smooth. Chill and serve. Serves 6-8.

Per serving (3 tbsp.): Calories 187 (81% from fat), Protein 5g, Carb. 4.4g, Total Fat 17.7g, Sodium 782mg, Dietary Fiber 1.27g

Vinegar & Oil Dressing

1/2 cup OLIVE OIL
1/2 tsp. GARLIC POWDER
1/2 tsp. ONION POWDER
1 GREEN PEPPER

1/2 tsp. BASIL
1/4 cup WATER
2 Tbsp. TAMARI

Combine all ingredients in blender and blend for 1 minute until smooth. Chill and serve. Serves 4.

Per serving (3 tbsp.): Calories 252 (95% from fat), Protein 1.21g, Carb. 2.05g, Total Fat 28g, Sodium 504mg, Dietary Fiber 0.4g

Miso Dressing

1 cup WATER
1/4 cup VEGETABLE OIL
1/8 cup RICE VINEGAR
1 Tbsp. TAHINI
dash CAYENNE
2 Tbsp. RICE SYRUP
1/2 ONION
3 Tbsp. YELLOW MISO
1 tsp. GARLIC POWDER

Combine all ingredients in a blender and blend well. Chill and serve.

Serves 3-4.

Per serving (3 tbsp.): Calories 235 (62% from fat), Protein 21.7g, Carb. 8g, Total Fat 22g, Sodium 639mg, Dietary Fiber 1.22.

Tahini Dressing

1 cup WATER
1/8 tsp. GARLIC POWDER
1 tsp. PEANUT BUTTER
1/2 cup TAHINI
1 Tbsp. TAMARI
dash CAYENNE
1/8 tsp. BASIL
1/2 tsp. OREGANO
dash SEA SALT
1/4 ONION

Combine all ingredients in a blender and blend until smooth. Chill and serve.

Serves 4-6.

Per serving (3 tbsp.): Calories 154 (73% from fat), Protein 5g, Carb.6.1g, Total Fat 13.6g, Sodium 239mg, Dietary Fiber 0.16.

SAUCES, GRAVIES, SPREADS & DIPS

Tomato-Mushroom Sauce

2 MUSHROOMS, sliced thin
2 Tbsp. SOY MARGARINE
2 Tbsp. SOY FLOUR
3 cups VEGETABLE STOCK
2 Tbsp. TOMATO SAUCE
1 tsp. NUTRITIONAL YEAST
1 Tbsp. TAMARI
dash BLACK PEPPER

Sauté mushroom in margarine, stirring frequently. Slowly add soy flour stirring constantly. Add boiling vegetable stock and remaining ingredients. Simmer for 30 minutes, stirring frequently.

Makes 3 - 3 1/2 cups.

Per 1/4 cup: Calories 21 (79% from fat), Protein 0.53g, Carb. 0.62g, Total Fat 1.94g, Sodium 116mg, Dietary Fiber 0.23g

Tomato Sauce

4 lg. TOMATOES, peeled
2 GARLIC CLOVES, crushed, diced
1/2 ONION, chopped
1/2 GREEN PEPPER, chopped
1 Tbsp. OLIVE OIL
1 Tbsp. OREGANO
1 Tbsp. TAMARI
dash RED PEPPER

Drop tomatoes in boiling water for 3 minutes, skin will peel away very easily. Sauté garlic onion and green pepper in oil until soft. Blend all ingredients together in a blender. Simmer mixture until thickness desired.

Makes 2 cups.

Per 1/4 cup: Calories 451 (30% from fat), Protein 11g, Carb. 74g, Total Fat 16.5g, Sodium 1073mg, Dietary Fiber 12.3g

Sweet & Sour Sauce

1 1/2 cups UNSWEETENED PINEAPPLE JUICE
1/2 cup DATE SUGAR
1/2 cup APPLE CIDER VINEGAR
1 tsp. GARLIC POWDER
2 Tbsp. SOY POWDER
1/4 cup TAMARI

Combine all ingredients in a saucepan on low to medium heat, stirring continuously until smooth and thick.

Makes 2 1/2 - 3 cups.

Per 1/4 cup: Calories 27 (6% from fat), Protein 1.1g, Carb. 7.7g, Total Fat 0.24g, Sodium 336mg, Dietary Fiber 0.19g

Banana-Pineapple Sauce

3 ripe BANANAS
1 cup fresh PINEAPPLE
1/2 cup APPLE JUICE
1 tsp. COCONUT FLAKES

Combine all ingredients in a blender and blend until smooth. Chill and serve. Great over fruit or your favorite morning delights, pancakes, french toast, etc.

Makes 2 cups.

Per 1/4 cup: Calories 63 (14% from fat), Protein 0.57g, Carb. 14.1g, Total Fat 1.04g, Sodium 6.9mg, Dietary Fiber 1.32g

Pasta Nut Sauce

1 1/2 Tbsp. SOY MARGARINE
1 Tbsp. SOY FLOUR
3 cups SOY MILK
1/2 cup WALNUTS, chopped fine
2 GARLIC CLOVES, crushed
2 BAY LEAVES
1 Tbsp. TAMARI
dash BLACK PEPPER
1/4 tsp. NUTMEG

Melt margarine in saucepan and slowly stir in flour till smooth. Add soy milk, nuts, garlic and bay leaves and cook for 5 minutes over low heat, stirring frequently. Let cool and add mixture to a blender. Add remaining ingredients and blend together until smooth. Return mixture to saucepan and simmer for 25 minutes, stirring frequently.

Makes 3 - 3 1/2 cups.

Per 1/4 cup: Calories 63 (70% from fat), Protein 3g, Carb. 2g, Total Fat 5.2g, Sodium 102mg, Dietary Fiber 0.9g

Carob Sauce

2 cups SOY MILK
2 Tbsp. SOY MARGARINE
8 Tbsp. CAROB POWDER
2 Tbsp. SORGHUM
1/2 tsp. DATE SUGAR
2 tsp. VANILLA

Mix ingredients in a saucepan over low heat. Cook, stirring frequently until thickened. Serve hot or cold.

Makes 2 - 2 1/2 cups.

Per 1/4 cup: Calories 65 (42% from fat), Protein 1.73g, Carb. 9.4g, Total Fat 3.6g, Sodium 44mg, Dietary Fiber 1.18g

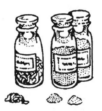

Margarine Lemon Sauce

4 oz. SOY MARGARINE
2 Tbsp. LEMON JUICE
1 Tbsp. PARSLEY
dash SEA SALT
dash PEPPER
1 tsp. OLIVE OIL

Melt margarine in small saucepan, add all remaining ingredients, stir well. Serve hot over green vegetables.

Makes 1/4 cup.

Per 1/4 cup: Calories 848 (99% from fat), Protein 0.21g, Carb. 2.25g, Total Fat 96g, Sodium 1226mg, Dietary Fiber 0.15g

Salsa

4 TOMATOES
2 tsp. CHILI POWDER
2 Tbsp. fresh CILANTRO
1/2 tsp. BLACK PEPPER
4 GREEN ONIONS
1 tsp. OREGANO
1 Tbsp. TAMARI

Combine all ingredients in a blender and blend until smooth. Chill and serve.

Makes 1 1/2 cups.

Per 1/4 cup: Calories 31.4 (17% from fat), Protein 1.7g, Carb. 6.4g, Total Fat 0.72g, Sodium 185mg, Dietary Fiber 1.45g

Green Salsa Sauce

1 ONION
1/2 cup PARSLEY
1 Tbsp. BASIL
1 Tbsp. DILL
1 tsp. LEMON JUICE
dash BLACK PEPPER
1 Tbsp. CHERVIL
1 LEMON PEEL
1 GARLIC CLOVE
3/4 cup OLIVE OIL
1 Tbsp. TAMARI

PARSLEY

Combine all ingredients and blend in a blender for 1 minute. Chill and serve.

Makes 1 cup.

Per 1/4 cup: Calories 385 (94% from fat), Protein 1.46g, Carb. 4.9g, Total Fat 42g, Sodium 259mg, Dietary Fiber 0.75g

Cheese Gravy

1/3 cup SOY FLOUR
1/2 cup NUTRITIONAL YEAST
1/4 cup VEGETABLE OIL
2 cups VEGETABLE STOCK
1 Tbsp. ONION POWDER
1 Tbsp. TAMARI

1 tsp. GARLIC
POWDER
1 tsp. OREGANO
1 tsp. BASIL
1/2 tsp. PAPRIKA

In a saucepan combine flour and yeast, stir oil into mixture forming a thick batter. Slowly stir in vegetable stock, stirring continuously until creamy. Add remaining ingredients, mix well and simmer until done.

Makes 2 1/2 - 3 cups.

Per 1/4 cup: Calories 65 (80% from fat), Protein 1.4g, Carb. 1.93g, Total Fat 6.1g, Sodium 102mg, Dietary Fiber 0.48g

Mushroom Gravy

2 Tbsp. SOY POWDER
1 tsp. NUTRITIONAL YEAST
2 cups WATER
4 ozs. MUSHROOMS, sliced
1 Tbsp. VEGETABLE OIL
4 Tbsp. TAMARI

Stir soy powder and yeast in water until smooth. Sauté mushrooms in vegetable oil and tamari until mushrooms are soft. Add liquid mixture stirring over low heat until desired thickness.

Makes 2 1/2 - 3 cups.

Per 1/4 cup: Calories 21.8 (64% from fat), Protein 1.22g, Carb. 0.88g, Total Fat 1.63g, Sodium 404mg, Dietary Fiber 0.27g

Shitake Sesame Mushroom Gravy

6 lg. fresh SHITAKE MUSHROOMS or 1 package dried
   SHITAKE MUSHROOMS
2 Tbsp. SESAME SEEDS
2 Tbsp. SESAME OIL
3 GARLIC CLOVES, minced
1 Tbsp. TAMARI
1 lg. ONION, sliced half moon style
1 GREEN BELL PEPPER, sliced
2 Tbsp. ARROWROOT
1 Tbsp. NUTRITIONAL YEAST
1 cup SOY MILK

If mushrooms are fresh, remove stems and slice thin. If mushrooms are dried, soak according to directions, drain and slice thin. Heat sesame seeds in dry saucepan until seeds are lightly golden. Add oil and garlic and sauté until garlic is lightly golden. Add tamari, mushrooms, onion and pepper, lower heat and cover for 5 minutes. Stir arrowroot and yeast into soy milk and stir slowly into sauté to form gravy. Delicious over rice or pasta.

Serves 4.

Per serving: Calories 200 (44% from fat), Protein 5.9g, Carb. 23.5g, Total Fat 10.5g, Sodium 273mg, Dietary Fiber 3.54g

Miso Tahini Spread

1/2 cup TAHINI
6 Tbsp. WATER
2 Tbsp. APPLE CIDER VINEGAR
1 tsp. SORGHUM
1 Tbsp. MISO

Combine all ingredients and blend thoroughly until creamy. Makes 3/4 cup.

Per 3/4 cup: Calories 734 (64% from fat), Protein 41g, Carb. 43g, Total Fat 66g, Sodium 770mg, Dietary Fiber 0.95g

Walnut Tofu Spread

1 (8 oz.) TOFU CAKE   **2 Tbsp. VEGETABLE OIL**
1/4 cup WALNUTS   **1/2 tsp. SEA SALT**
3 Tbsp. LEMON JUICE   **1 tsp. SORGHUM**

Drain tofu and blend all ingredients in a blender until creamy. Makes 1 1/2 cups.

Per 1/2 cup: Calories 215 (74% from fat), Protein 9.4g, Carb. 5.3g, Total Fat 19g, Sodium 385mg, Dietary Fiber 0.59g

Tofu Butter Nut Spread

1 (12 oz.) TOFU CAKE, drained
1 Tbsp. BROWN RICE SYRUP
2 tsp. LEMON JUICE
1/2 cup DRIED CURRANTS
4 Tbsp. CASHEW BUTTER
1/2 tsp. SEA SALT

Combine all ingredients in a food processor or a blender and blend together until smooth. Keep refrigerated. Makes 1 1/2 - 2 cups.

Per 1/2 cup: Calories 184 (47% from fat), Protein 9g, Carb. 15.7g, Total Fat 10g, Sodium 234mg, Dietary Fiber 0.36g

Zesty Garden Dip

3 CELERY STALKS, diced
1/4 cup CILANTRO, chopped
6 mild GREEN CHILIES, diced
2 cups cooked PEAS, cooled
1 Tbsp. LEMON JUICE
1 (12 oz.) TOFU CAKE, drained
1 1/2 tsp. CUMIN
1/4 tsp. BLACK PEPPER
dash SEA SALT

Combine all ingredients in food processor or blender for 30 seconds. Serve chilled. Great dip for vegetables. Makes 2 cups.

Per 1/2 cup: Calories 63 (27% from fat), Protein 4.6g, Carb. 8.3g, Total Fat 2.07g, Sodium 16mg, Dietary Fiber 3.4g

Guacamole

2 AVOCADOS, mashed
1/2 TOMATO, diced fine
1/2 ONION, diced fine
1 Tbsp. LEMON JUICE
1 tsp. SPIKE®
1/2 cup WATER
1/4 tsp. CUMIN
1/4 tsp. CHILI POWDER
1 tsp. GARLIC POWDER
1 Tbsp. TAMARI

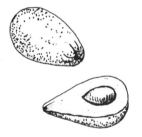

In a large bowl, mash avocados well and combine the remaining ingredients. Mix thoroughly until smooth. Great with chips and crackers. Makes 1 to 1 1/2 cups.

Per 1/2 cup: Calories 114 (73% from fat), Protein 1.88g, Carb. 6.4g, Total Fat 10.1g, Sodium 371mg, Dietary Fiber 1.58g

Sea Seasoning & Tofu Dip

1 (8 oz.) TOFU CAKE, drained
2 Tbsp. NORI with GINGER
2 Tbsp. TAMARI
1/2 tsp. VEGETABLE OIL
dash LEMON JUICE

Combine all ingredients in a blender and blend till smooth.

Makes 1 1/2 cups.

Per 1/2 cup: Calories 80 (49% from fat), Protein 8.6g, Carb. 2.67g, Total Fat 4.8g, Sodium 681mg, Dietary Fiber 0.1g

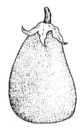

Eggplant Dip

1 sm. EGGPLANT
1/8 cup VEGETABLE OIL
1/8 cup BROWN RICE VINEGAR
1 TOMATO
1 GREEN ONION
1 tsp. CHILI POWDER
1/2 tsp. OREGANO
1/2 tsp. BASIL

Peel, cube and cook eggplant till soft. Combine all ingredients in a blender and blend until creamy. Cover and chill 2 hours.

Serves 5. (Makes 1 cup.)

Per serving: Calories 62 (77% from fat), Protein 0.64g, Carb. 3.1g, Total Fat 5.6g, Sodium 8.6mg, Dietary Fiber 0.49g

Vegetable Dip

1 cup NUT BUTTER
2 TOMATOES, peeled
1 sm. ONION, grated
1 GREEN ONION, diced
1/4 cup VEGETABLE OIL
dash PAPRIKA
dash SEA SALT

Combine all ingredients into a blender and blend until smooth. Chill and serve.

Makes 2 cups.

Per 1/2 cup: Calories 265 (75% from fat), Protein 9.6g, Carb. 8.4g, Total Fat 23.3g, Sodium 157mg, Dietary Fiber 3.1g

Hummus Dip

4 cups CHICK PEAS,
    cooked till tender
3 GARLIC CLOVES
4 Tbsp. TAHINI
1 tsp. OLIVE OIL
1 tsp. PARSLEY
2 Tbsp. LEMON JUICE
5 Tbsp. TAMARI
1/2 tsp. PEPPER

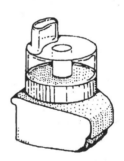

Combine all ingredients into a food processor and blend till smooth. Great spread for crackers, bread, etc.

Makes 2 cups.

Per 1/2 cup: Calories 179 (26% from fat), Protein 7.6g, Carb. 26.6g, Total Fat 5.4g, Sodium 886mg, Dietary Fiber 3.56g

Scallion Chive Dip

1 (12 oz.) TOFU CAKE, drained
1 Tbsp. BROWN RICE VINEGAR
2 SCALLIONS, diced
1/4 tsp. BLACK PEPPER
1/2 cup CHIVES, diced
1 Tbsp. TAMARI
1/2 tsp. GARLIC POWDER
dash SEA SALT

Set scallions and chives aside. Blend all other ingredients in a blender till creamy. Stir scallions and chives into creamy mixture.

Makes 2 cups.

Per 1/2 cup: Calories 63 (46% from fat), Protein 6.7g, Carb. 2.6g, Total Fat 3.6g, Sodium 212mg, Dietary Fiber 0.3g

Onion Green Bean Dip

1 (8 oz.) TOFU CAKE, drained
1/2 cup GREEN BEANS, cooked and drained
1 ONION
1 tsp. SEA SALT
2 Tbsp. roasted SUNFLOWER SEEDS
2 tsp. ONION MAGIC®
2 Tbsp. VEGETABLE OIL
2 Tbsp. LEMON JUICE
dash PAPRIKA

Combine all ingredients in a blender and blend until smooth and creamy.

Serves 3. Makes 2 1/4 cups.

Per serving: Calories 270 (70% from fat), Protein 12g, Carb. 9.7g, Total Fat 22.5g, Sodium 882mg, Dietary Fiber 2.07g

MAIN DISHES

Pasta Primavera

1/2 lb. SPINACH SPAGHETTI
1 cup BROCCOLI FLORETS
1/2 cup CARROTS, sliced
3/4 cup PEAS
1 cup CAULIFLOWER
1/2 cup VEGETABLE STOCK
1 cup SOY MILK
1/8 cup NUTRITIONAL YEAST
1/4 tsp. BLACK PEPPER
1/4 tsp. GARLIC POWDER
3 Tbsp. SOY MARGARINE
dash NUTMEG

Prepare pasta according to package directions and drain. Steam vegetables in vegetable stock in a large saucepan until vegetables are tender, drain and set aside. Combine remaining ingredients in saucepan over medium heat, stirring for about 5 minutes. Add pasta and steamed vegetables to sauce, mixing well. Serves 4.

Per serving: Calories 358 (31% from fat), Protein 12.7g, Carb. 50g, Total Fat 12.3g, Sodium 147mg, Dietary Fiber 5.7g

Tempeh Cabbage Casserole

1 1/2 cups TEMPEH
1 Tbsp. VEGETABLE OIL
1/4 cup ONION, diced
4 fresh MUSHROOMS, sliced
1/2 cup GREEN PEPPER, diced
1/2 cup CELERY, dic
1 1/2 cups TOMATO SAUCE
1 1/2 cups TOFU
4 Tbsp. NUTRITIONAL YEAST
4 Tbsp. TAMARI
1 tsp. GARLIC POWDER
1 tsp. ONION POWDER
dash BLACK PEPPER
4 Tbsp. VEGETABLE OIL
1 head CABBAGE, shredded
1 1/2 cups SOYMAGE®, grated

Sauté tempeh in 1 tablespoon vegetable oil with onion, mushrooms, green pepper and celery until tempeh is cooked. Add tomato sauce. In blender, blend tofu, spices and oil until smooth. Layer 1/3 tomato sauce, 1/3 cabbage, 1/3 sauté mixture and 1/3 soymage in large casserole. Continue layering with the soymage as the top layer. Bake at 350 degrees for 1 hour.

Serves 4-6.

Per serving: Calories 491 (48% from fat), Protein 29g, Carb. 40g, Total Fat 28g, Sodium 1621mg, Dietary Fiber 5.7g

Beans & Onions

2 ONIONS, sliced
3 Tbsp. VEGETABLE OIL
2 RED BELL PEPPERS, diced
1 GREEN CHILI PEPPER, diced
1 Tbsp. TAMARI
1 tsp. grated COCONUT
1/2 tsp. TURMERIC
1/2 cup TOMATO SAUCE
1 Tbsp. BROWN RICE SYRUP
2 cups cooked KIDNEY BEANS

Sauté onions in oil until lightly brown. Add peppers, tamari, coconut and turmeric, stirring and frying for about 3 minutes. Add tomato sauce and syrup, continue stirring and frying for 3 minutes. Add beans, just to heat them thoroughly, stirring to mix well.

Serves 4.

Per serving: Calories 274 (37% from fat), Protein 10g, Carb. 33g, Total Fat 11.2g, Sodium 754mg, Dietary Fiber 12.2g

Greek Style Beans

2 1/2 cups fresh GREEN
    BEANS, sliced
2 cups TOMATO SAUCE
1 sm. ONION, diced

1 Tbsp. TAMARI
1 tsp. OREGANO
dash NUTMEG
dash CINNAMON

Combine all ingredients in crockpot. Set on low and cook for 3 hours.

Serves 4.

Per serving: Calories 65 (5% from fat), Protein 3.4g, Carb. 15g, Total Fat 0.43g, Sodium 1438mg, Dietary Fiber 3.8g

Vegetable Burgers

1 Tbsp. VEGETABLE OIL
2 GREEN CHILI PEPPERS, diced
1 ONION, diced
2 CARROTS, diced
1/2 cup TEMPEH
1 cup mashed POTATOES
2 GREEN PEPPERS, diced
3 GARLIC CLOVES, diced
1/2 bunch PARSLEY, chopped
4 Tbsp. TAMARI
1/2 cup WHOLE WHEAT BREAD crumbs
1/2 cup PEANUT OIL

Sauté peppers, onions and carrots in oil until soft. Add all remaining ingredients to mixture and blend well. Divide mixture into 5 burgers, shape and fry in 1/2 cup peanut oil.

Serves 5.

Per serving: Calories 450 (56% from fat), Protein 9g, Carb. 41.5g, Total Fat 29g, Sodium 1026mg, Dietary Fiber 4.4g

Sprout Cutlets

2 cups SUNFLOWER SPROUTS
2 cups BEAN SPROUTS
1 ONION, diced
1 GREEN BELL PEPPER, diced
4 GARLIC CLOVES, diced
3 slices WHOLE WHEAT BREAD
1/2 cup CORN FLAKE CRUMBS
1/4 cup PEANUT OIL
2 Tbsp. TAMARI
2 POTATOES, cooked and mashed
2 Tbsp. LEMON JUICE

Steam sprouts until soft. Sauté onion, peppers and garlic in 1/2 of peanut oil and tamari until tender. Chop bread into small pieces and mix well with sautéed vegetables. Add steamed sprouts, mashed potatoes and lemon juice, stirring until well blended. Shape mixture into 6 cutlets and roll in corn flake crumbs. Fry on both sides in peanut oil until brown. Serve with your favorite sauce.

Serves 6.

Per serving: Calories 264 (44% from fat), Protein 7.8g, Carb. 31.6g, Total Fat 13.8g, Sodium 670mg, Dietary Fiber 3.8g

Zucchini-Potato Bake

2 Tbsp. VEGETABLE OIL
1 GREEN BELL PEPPER, diced
2 ONIONS, sliced
2 GARLIC CLOVES, diced
1 ZUCCHINI, sliced thin
2 cups TOMATO SAUCE
1 Tbsp. TAMARI
1 tsp. BASIL
dash CAYENNE PEPPER
3 POTATOES, peeled, sliced and baked
1/2 cup SOYMAGE®, grated
2 Tbsp. NUTRITIONAL YEAST

Sauté in oil, peppers, onion, garlic and zucchini until tender. Spread 1/2 cup of the tomato sauce in casserole dish. Add remaining tomato sauce, tamari, basil and cayenne to sauté. Layer 1/2 of the potatoes on top of tomato sauce in casserole dish, then cover with 1/2 of the soymage and 1/2 of tomato sauté mixture. Layer the second 1/2 of potatoes and the remainder of tomato sauté mixture and top with remainder of soymage. Sprinkle with nutritional yeast. Bake at 350 degrees for 30 minutes.

Serves 4.

Per serving: Calories 380 (23% from fat), Protein 10.8g, Carb. 66g, Total Fat 10g, Sodium 1143mg, Dietary Fiber 8g

Rice-Millet Loaf

2 CARROTS, diced
3 GARLIC CLOVES, diced
2 Tbsp. VEGETABLE OIL
1 Tbsp. TAMARI
2 cups TOMATO SAUCE
1 cup cooked BROWN RICE
2 cups cooked MILLET
3 GREEN ONIONS, diced
1/4 cup BEAN SPROUTS
2 Tbsp. TAHINI
1 tsp. BASIL
1/4 cup WHEAT GERM
1/8 cup NUTRITIONAL YEAST

Sauté carrots and garlic in oil and tamari until carrots are tender. Set aside 1/2 cup of tomato sauce. Mix rice and millet together, add all other ingredients to rice mixture, blend well. Mold mixture into loaf and put in baking dish. Cover top of loaf with the tomato sauce that was set aside. Bake at 350 degrees for 30-40 minutes.

Serves 4-6.

Per serving: Calories 331 (29% from fat), Protein 11g, Carb. 53g, Total Fat 11.4g, Sodium 813mg, Dietary Fiber 8.4g

Cabbage & Noodle Melt

2 ONIONS, sliced
3 GARLIC CLOVES, minced
2 Tbsp. VEGETABLE OIL
2 GREEN BELL PEPPERS, sliced
1 head CABBAGE, shredded
1/2 tsp. PAPRIKA
1/4 cup TAMARI
2 cups cooked NOODLES
1/3 cup SOY MARGARINE
1 cup SOYMAGE®, grated

Sauté onions and garlic in vegetable oil until onions are soft. Add peppers and sauté 4 more minutes. Add cabbage and seasonings, reduce heat to low, cover and cook until cabbage is soft. Stir in noodles, mixing well. Pour into serving bowl. Melt margarine and grated soymage in small saucepan. Pour over cabbage and noodles.

Serves 3-4.

Per serving: Calories 654 (51% from fat), Protein 21.5g, Carb. 62g, Total Fat 39g, Sodium 2040mg, Dietary Fiber 7g

Swiss Chard Rolls

Stuffing

1 cup cooked BROWN RICE	1 ONION, diced
2 Tbsp. TAMARI	1/2 cup crumbled TEMPEH
1 cup soaked BULGUR	3 CELERY STALKS, diced
2 GARLIC CLOVES, diced	3 Tbsp. VEGETABLE OIL

Tofu Mixture

1 (8 oz.) TOFU CAKE	1/4 cup TAMARI
1/4 cup VEGETABLE OIL	1/2 tsp. GARLIC POWDER
1/4 cup NUTRITIONAL YEAST	1/2 tsp. ONION POWDER

Sauce

1 cup TOMATO SAUCE	dash FRUCTOSE
1 Tbsp. SORGHUM	12 SWISS CHARD
2 tsp. LEMON JUICE	LEAVES

Stuffing: Soak bulgur one hour. Combine with rice and tamari in a large bowl. Sauté garlic, onion, tempeh and celery in vegetable oil until vegetables are soft and add to rice mixture, stirring until well blended.

Tofu Mixture: Blend all ingredients in blender until smooth.

Sauce: Simmer all ingredients in saucepan until sauce is hot. Add 1/4 of sauce to tofu mixture. Spread 1/2 of remaining sauce on bottom of casserole dish.

Put equal amounts of stuffing and tofu mixture onto each swiss chard leaf, roll and place in casserole dish. Cover rolls with remaining sauce. Bake at 350 degrees for 20 minutes.

Serves 6.

Per serving: Calories 364 (41% from fat), Protein 15.2g, Carb. 42g, Total Fat 17.6g, Sodium 1359mg, Dietary Fiber 6g

Vegetable Loaf

8 fresh MUSHROOMS
1/4 cup VEGETABLE STOCK
1/4 cup TOMATO JUICE
3 CARROTS
1 BEET
2 CELERY STALKS
2 POTATOES
2 ONIONS
1 tsp. PARSLEY
1 tsp. BASIL
2 Tbsp. WALNUTS, chopped
1 Tbsp. SUNFLOWER SEEDS
1 Tbsp. VEGETABLE OIL
2 Tbsp. SUNFLOWER MEAL
2 tsp. NUTRITIONAL YEAST
1/2 cup grated SOYMAGE
1 cup WHOLE WHEAT BREAD crumbs
2 Tbsp. TAMARI
3 GARLIC CLOVES
1 tsp. THYME

Combine all ingredients in food processor and chop fine. Oil baking pan and form mixture into loaf. Bake at 350 degrees for 45-55 minutes.

Serves 5.

Per serving: Calories 284 (33% from fat), Protein 12g, Carb. 38g, Total Fat 10.8g, Sodium 721mg, Dietary Fiber 3.8g

Mixed Vegetable Stew

3 GARLIC CLOVES, diced
1 Tbsp. SESAME SEEDS
1 EGGPLANT, peeled, chopped
3 Tbsp. VEGETABLE OIL
2 cups VEGETABLE JUICE
3 CARROTS, diced
1 ZUCCHINI, sliced
12 fresh MUSHROOMS, sliced
1/2 cup TOMATO SAUCE
1/2 tsp. OREGANO
1/4 tsp. MARJORAM

Sauté garlic, sesame seeds and eggplant in vegetable oil for 4 minutes. Add juice, carrots, zucchini and continue cooking for 4 minutes. Add mushrooms, tomato sauce and seasonings. Lower heat and simmer for 12 minutes. Serve over couscous, rice or pasta.

Serves 4-6.

Per cup: Calories 137 (57% from fat), Protein 2.7g, Carb. 13g, Total Fat 9.4g, Sodium 516 mg, Dietary Fiber 3.07g

Seitan Peppers & Onions

3 ONIONS, sliced
4 GREEN BELL PEPPERS, sliced
1/2 cup SEITAN, finely chopped
2 GARLIC CLOVES, diced
2 Tbsp. SESAME SEEDS
1 Tbsp. VEGETABLE OIL
3 Tbsp. TAMARI
1 tsp. BASIL

Sauté seitan, onions, bell peppers, garlic and sesame seeds in vegetable oil until vegetables are soft and sesame seeds are golden brown. Add spices and stir well. Serve over rice.

Serves 3-4.

Per serving: Calories 374 (17% from fat), Protein 21g, Carb. 70g, Total Fat 8.5g, Sodium 1047mg, Dietary Fiber 9.8g

Mashed Potatoes with Spinach

6 POTATOES, peeled and quartered
1 bunch SPINACH, remove stems
3 Tbsp. SOY MARGARINE
1 Tbsp. TAMARI
dash BLACK PEPPER

Place 3 quarts of water in large pot and boil potatoes until soft; drain and mash. Steam spinach until tender, drain. Add steamed spinach to mashed potatoes with margarine and seasonings, mix well.

Serves 4-6.

Per serving: Calories 177 (35% from fat), Protein 4.2g, Carb. 25.7g, Total Fat 7.1g, Sodium 314mg, Dietary Fiber 1.72g

Linguine a la Walnuts

12 ozs. WHOLE WHEAT LINGUINE
3 lg. ONIONS, sliced
4 Tbsp. SESAME SEEDS
2 GARLIC CLOVES, minced
1/2 cup SOY MARGARINE
2 Tbsp. VEGETABLE OIL
1 Tbsp. TAMARI
dash BLACK PEPPER
1 Tbsp. ground WALNUTS

Prepare linguine as directed on package. Sauté onions, sesame seeds and garlic in oil until onions are tender. Add margarine, spices and walnuts, stirring well. Add linguine and toss until coated with sauce. Serves 6.

Per serving: Calories 459 (47% from fat), Protein 10.3g, Carb. 51g, Total Fat 24.4g, Sodium 375mg, Dietary Fiber 3.46g

Spinach Eggplant Sauté

1 EGGPLANT, peeled, 1/2 inch cubes
2 GARLIC CLOVES, diced
1 Tbsp. SESAME SEEDS
2 MILD GREEN CHILES, sliced thin
1 Tbsp. VEGETABLE OIL
1 lg. bunch SPINACH, stems removed
3/4 cup WATER
1 tsp. BASIL
1 tsp. OREGANO
1 Tbsp. TAMARI

Sauté eggplant, garlic, sesame seeds and chiles in oil. When eggplant is tender add remaining ingredients. Cover and simmer 5 minutes. Serves 5.

Per serving: Calories 85 (47% from fat), Protein 4.5g, Carb. 8.4g, Total Fat 5g, Sodium 319mg, Dietary Fiber 3.86g

Chop Suey

4 MUSHROOMS, sliced
1/2 cup JICAMA, sliced thin
4 ONIONS, chopped
4 celery stalks, CHOPPED
2 Tbsp. OLIVE OIL

1 cup BEAN SPROUTS
3 cups BAMBOO SHOOTS
8 CHESTNUTS, sliced thin
1 tsp. ARROWROOT
1 Tbsp. GARLIC POWDER

Sauté mushrooms, jicama, onions and celery in oil about 7 minutes. Add sprouts, bamboo shoots and chestnuts and continue sauté for 5 minutes. Add arrowroot and garlic powder mixing well.

Serves 4-6.

Per serving: Calories 185 (29% from fat), Protein 5.9g, Carb. 29.4g, Total Fat 6.5g, Sodium 64mg, Dietary Fiber 7.2g

Vegetable Kabob

2 GREEN BELL PEPPERS, cut 6 wedges
2 RED BELL PEPPERS, cut 6 wedges
12 MUSHROOMS
12 PEARL ONIONS
12 CHERRY TOMATOES
1 Tbsp. KETCHUP, no sugar
1 Tbsp. TAMARI
1 Tbsp. VEGETABLE OIL
1 tsp. BASIL
1/2 tsp. OREGANO

Skewer peppers, mushrooms, onions and tomatoes. Mix tamari, oil and spices and brush on vegetables. Barbecue 4 minutes each side.

Serves 4.

Per serving: Calories 98 (36% from fat), Protein 3.44g, Carb. 13.8g, Total Fat 4.3g, Sodium 579mg, Dietary Fiber 4.5g

Eggplant au Gratin

1 lg. EGGPLANT
1 ONION, diced
1/2 cup CARROTS, diced
1/2 cup CELERY, diced
2 GARLIC CLOVES, diced
2 Tbsp. VEGETABLE OIL
1 Tbsp. TAMARI
1 tsp. PAPRIKA
1/8 cup ground WALNUTS
3 Tbsp. SOY MARGARINE
1/2 cup grated SOYMAGE
1/4 cup WHOLE WHEAT BREAD crumbs

Cut eggplant in half, scoop out center to 1/4 inch of outer skin and set aside. Dice scooped out eggplant and sauté with onion, carrots, celery and garlic in oil until vegetables are tender. Add spices and walnuts, stirring constantly. Spoon mixture into eggplant shells. Place shells in baking pan. Melt margarine and soymage. Spread bread crumbs over eggplant and pour margarine on top. Bake in slow oven for 25-30 minutes.

Serves 4.

Per serving: Calories 256 (70% from fat), Protein 6.4g, Carb. 13.6g, Total Fat 20.6g, Sodium 546mg, Dietary Fiber 1.62g

Vegetable Brown Rice

2 ONIONS, chopped
3 CELERY STALKS, diced
3 CARROTS, diced
2 GARLIC CLOVES, diced
2 Tbsp. VEGETABLE OIL
12 oz. SPINACH, stems
   removed

3 cups cooked BROWN
   RICE
1 tsp. PAPRIKA
1/2 cup TAMARI
3 Tbsp. PEANUTS

Sauté onions, celery, carrots and garlic in vegetable oil until vegetables are tender. Add spinach and continue to sauté until spinach is cooked. Blend mixture into the brown rice and add seasonings and peanuts.

Serves 4-6.

Per serving: Calories 294 (28% from fat), Protein 10.5g, Carb. 45g, Total Fat 9.4g, Sodium 1724mg, Dietary Fiber 6.4g

Tofu Carrot Loaf

1 (12 oz.) TOFU CAKE
1 cup CARROTS,
   chopped, steamed
1/2 cup SOY MILK
1 cup WHOLE WHEAT
   BREAD crumbs

1/2 cup WALNUTS, chopped
1 ONION, diced
1 Tbsp. OIL
1 tsp. BASIL
1 Tbsp. TAMARI
1/2 cup grated SOYMAGE®

Set soymage aside. Blend all other ingredients in blender until smooth. Pour mixture into an oiled loaf-style baking dish. Sprinkle soymage on top of loaf. Bake at 350 degrees for 30 minutes.

Serves 3-4.

Per serving: Calories 491 (49% from fat), Protein 26.4g, Carb. 39.5g, Total Fat 28g, Sodium 780mg, Dietary Fiber 4.15g

Couscous & Noodles

1/2 lb. WHOLE WHEAT NOODLES
1 1/2 ONIONS, sliced
2 GARLIC CLOVES, minced
1 Tbsp. SESAME SEEDS
2 Tbsp. VEGETABLE OIL
2 Tbsp. TAMARI
1 cup fresh MUSHROOMS, sliced
1/2 cup SOY MARGARINE
1 tsp. BASIL
2 cups cooked COUSCOUS

Prepare noodles following package directions. Sauté onions, garlic and sesame seeds. When onions are transparent, add mushrooms and continue to sauté until mushrooms are soft. Add margarine and basil. When margarine has melted, pour sauté over noodles and mix well. Serve over couscous.

Serves 4.

Per serving: Calories 707 (40% from fat), Protein 16.5g, Carb. 89g, Total Fat 32g, Sodium 786mg, Dietary Fiber 3.65g

Rainbow Tofu Bake

1 ONION, diced
1 BEET, sliced
1 CARROT, sliced
1/2 cup BROCCOLI, chopped
2 CELERY STALKS, diced
1 RED BELL PEPPER, chopped
1 Tbsp. VEGETABLE OIL
2 (12 oz.) TOFU CAKES
3/4 cup WHOLE WHEAT BREAD crumbs
1 Tbsp. TAMARI
1/2 tsp. ONION POWDER
3/4 cup NUTRITIONAL YEAST
1/2 cup TAHINI
1/2 tsp. TURMERIC
1 tsp. BASIL
1/2 tsp. OREGANO

Sauté onion, beet, carrot, broccoli, celery and pepper in vegetable oil until tender. Mash tofu in bowl and blend in sautéed vegetables and the remaining ingredients until well blended. Oil a loaf-type baking dish and pour in the mixture. Bake at 350 degrees for 35-40 minutes.

Serves 6.

Per serving: Calories 265 (54% from fat), Protein 11.6g, Carb. 21g, Total Fat 17g, Sodium 320mg, Dietary Fiber 1.7g

Eggplant Burgers

3 ONIONS, diced
4 CELERY STALKS, diced
2 GARLIC CLOVES, minced
2 Tbsp. VEGETABLE OIL
2 EGGPLANTS, peeled and ground
1 cup ground WALNUTS
1 cup WHOLE WHEAT BREAD crumbs
2 Tbsp. TAMARI
1/8 cup WHOLE WHEAT FLOUR
1/2 cup TOMATO SAUCE

Sauté onions, celery and garlic in vegetable oil until vegetables are soft. Stir in all remaining ingredients except the tomato sauce. Form mixture into 6-8 burgers and shallow fry in oil until brown on both sides. Just before done add 1 tablespoon of tomato sauce to each burger and continue frying for 3 more minutes.

Serves 6-8.

Per serving: Calories 254 (50% from fat), Protein 8.6g, Carb. 25g, Total Fat 15g, Sodium 537mg, Dietary Fiber 3.5g

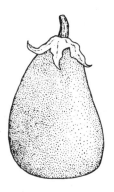

Miso Macaroni

10 oz. WHOLE WHEAT MACARONI
1 ONION, diced
1 GARLIC CLOVE, diced
1/2 cup BROCCOLI, chopped
1 Tbsp. VEGETABLE OIL
3/4 cup VEGETABLE STOCK
1/4 cup MISO
1 tsp. TAMARI
1 tsp. OREGANO
1 Tbsp. NUTRITIONAL YEAST
1/2 cup SOY MARGARINE

Cook whole wheat macaroni as directed on package instructions. Sauté onion, celery, garlic and broccoli in vegetable oil until vegetables are tender. Let vegetables cool. Add vegetable stock, miso and spices in saucepan. Stir over low heat until hot. When miso mixture has cooled, add this mixture to the blender along with the sautéed vegetables and blend until smooth. Pour over macaroni.

Serves 6.

Per serving: Calories 333 (40% from fat), Protein 21.g, Carb. 42g, Total Fat 19g, Sodium 689mg, Dietary Fiber 5.6g

Tempeh Spinach Lasagna

16 oz. WHOLE WHEAT LASAGNA NOODLES
1 lg. bunch SPINACH, stems removed
1 cup TEMPEH, crumbled
3 Tbsp. VEGETABLE OIL
2 Tbsp. TAMARI
2 (8 oz.) TOFU CAKES
2 Tbsp. NUTRITIONAL YEAST
2 Tbsp. GARLIC POWDER
1 Tbsp. ONION POWDER
dash SEA SALT
1 tsp. BASIL
1 tsp. OREGANO
1 cup grated SOYMAGE®
3 cups TOMATO SAUCE

Cook lasagna noodles as per package instructions and set aside. Steam spinach for 10 minutes and set aside. Sauté crumbled tempeh in 1 tablespoon of oil and tamari in saucepan until brown. Mash 1 cake of tofu in bowl and add spices and blend until smooth and creamy to make tofu mixture. Add the other cake of tofu, 2 tablespoons oil, 1 tablespoon water and grated soymage in blender to make tofu topping. Layer 5 or 6 times in oblong baking dish. Begin to layer: sauce, noodles, tempeh, spinach, tofu mixture. Fill baking dish and cover with tofu topping. Bake at 350 degrees for 1 hour.

Serves 8-10.

Per serving: Calories 261 (36% from fat), Protein 16.6g, Carb. 28.6g, Total Fat 11.4g, Sodium 866mg, Dietary Fiber 4.7g

Rice Casserole

1 (8 oz.) TOFU CAKE, mashed
1 ONION, diced
2 CARROTS, diced
1 RED BELL PEPPER, diced
1 tsp. VEGETABLE OIL
2 ZUCCHINI, chopped
8 ozs. MUSHROOMS, sliced
4 cups cooked BROWN RICE
1 BEET, diced
1 Tbsp. GARLIC POWDER
1 Tbsp. MARGARINE
1 tsp. NUTRITIONAL YEAST
1 Tbsp. TAMARI
1 cup WATER
8 oz. SOYMAGE®, grated
dash BLACK PEPPER
1 tsp. GARLIC POWDER
1 tsp. PAPRIKA

Sauté onions, carrots and pepper in vegetable oil for 10 minutes. Add zucchini and mushrooms and cook for 8 more minutes. Add all ingredients in large bowl and mix well. Pour mixture into oiled casserole, cover with foil and bake at 350 degrees for 45 minutes.

Serves 6.

Per serving: Calories 348 (31% from fat), Protein 17.2g, Carb. 45g, Total Fat 12.4g, Sodium 679mg, Dietary Fiber 4.9g

Curried Sauté

1 bunch BROCCOLI
1 head CAULIFLOWER
1 cup VEGETABLE STOCK
2 lg. ONIONS, sliced
4 GARLIC CLOVES, diced

1 1/2 cup MUSHROOMS, sliced
2 Tbsp. VEGETABLE OIL
3 Tbsp. TAMARI
1/2 tsp. CURRY POWDER

Cut the broccoli and cauliflower into bite-sized pieces and steam in vegetable stock until tender. Sauté onions, garlic and mushrooms in saucepan until golden brown. Add tamari, steamed vegetables and continue to sauté for 3 more minutes. Add spices and cook for 3 minutes.

Serves 6.

Per serving: Calories 117 (35% from fat), Protein 5.9g, Carb. 15.6g, Total Fat 5.1g, Sodium 539mg, Dietary Fiber 2.9g

Italian Lima Beans

1 ONION, chopped
2 BELL PEPPERS, chopped
2 GARLIC CLOVES, minced
1 tsp. VEGETABLE OIL

1 tsp. BASIL
1 tsp. OREGANO
1 tsp. TAMARI
1 cup TOMATO SAUCE
3 cups LIMA BEANS, cooked

Sauté onion, peppers and garlic until tender. Add spices and tomato sauce, sauté 3 minutes more. Add cooked lima beans and sautéed mixture in bowl, stirring until well blended.

Serves 4-6.

Per serving: Calories 164 (8% from fat), Protein 11g, Carb. 31g, Total Fat 1.55g, Sodium 404mg, Dietary Fiber 10.3g

Fantastic Stir Fry

2 Tbsp. SESAME SEEDS
2 Tbsp. SESAME OIL
8 ozs. MUSHROOMS, sliced
2 Tbsp. GINGER ROOT, grated
3 CLOVES GARLIC, minced
1 lg. ONION, sliced
2 ozs. SNOW PEAS
1 RED or YELLOW BELL PEPPER
1 stalk BROCCOLI, chopped
4 stalks BOK CHOY, chopped
2 Tbsp. TAMARI
1 tsp. FENNEL SEEDS
1/2 cup WATER
2 Tbsp. ARROWROOT
1 Tbsp. NUTRITIONAL YEAST

Roast sesame seeds in dry skillet or wok over medium high heat until golden brown. Add mushrooms, ginger root, garlic and 1 tablespoon sesame oil. Stir fry until garlic and mushrooms are golden brown. Remove from skillet and set aside. In skillet add other tablespoon of sesame oil and onion, stir fry 2 minutes, add all remaining vegetables, tamari and fennel seeds. Cover and lower heat for 5 minutes. Mix water, arrowroot and yeast together. Push vegetables in skillet to the sides, leaving a hole in the middle to add water/arrowroot mixture to natural vegetable juices. Stir liquids together and let liquid thicken. Stir in mushrooms and garlic. Serve over brown rice.

Serves 4-6.

Per serving: Calories 125 (52% from fat), Protein 4.1g, Carb. 11.8g, Total Fat 7.7g, Sodium 435mg, Dietary Fiber 2.4g

Tofu-Nut Stir Fry

1 (12 oz.) TOFU CAKE, cubed 3/4 inch
1/2 cup TAMARI
1 Tbsp. VEGETABLE OIL
2 GARLIC CLOVES, diced
4 lg. ONIONS, diced
1 BELL PEPPER, sliced
3 CELERY STALKS, sliced
1 cup WATER CHESTNUTS, sliced
1 Tbsp. GINGER ROOT, grated
2 cups cold WATER
2 Tbsp. ARROWROOT POWDER
1/2 cup roasted CASHEWS

Marinate tofu pieces in tamari for 1 hour. Sauté in oil and brown tofu on all sides, set aside. Sauté garlic, onions, bell pepper, celery, chestnuts and ginger root until vegetables are tender. Mix cold water and arrowroot in separate bowl until smooth. When vegetables are done, add arrowroot mixture over them and simmer until sauce is thickened. Put vegetables in serving bowl and top with tofu and cashews. Serve over grains.

Serves 4-6.

Per serving: Calories 275 (40% from fat), Protein 13.5g, Carb. 30g, Total Fat 13g, Sodium 1753mg, Dietary Fiber 3.56g

SIDE DISHES

Rice Salad

1 1/2 cups WATER
2 Tbsp. CANOLA OIL
2 GREEN ONIONS, diced
1 CARROT, diced
1 1/2 cups cooked
**   BROWN RICE**
1/2 RED BELL PEPPER,
**   diced**

Sauté in oil, onions and carrot until soft, add remaining vegetables and continue to sauté until all vegetables are tender. In a large bowl, mix well the sautéed vegetables and all remaining ingredients, saving the cashews to garnish the top of the salad. Chill and serve.

Serves 4-6.

Per serving: Calories 163 (41% from fat), Protein 3.5g, Carb. 21g, Total Fat 7.7g, Sodium 327mg, Dietary Fiber 2.73g

Tomato Corn Stir

1/4 lb. OKRA
2 cups fresh CORN KERNELS
4 TOMATOES, peeled, diced
1/2 cup ONION, diced
1 SWEET PEPPER, diced
1/4 cup SOY MARGARINE
dash SEA SALT
dash BLACK PEPPER
1 tsp. ONION POWDER
1 Tbsp. TAMARI

Sauté onion and pepper in saucepan in margarine until tender. Add remaining ingredients and simmer for 20 minutes, stirring occasionally. Serves 4-6.

Per serving: Calories 204 (42% from fat), Protein 5g, Carb. 28g, Total Fat 10.6g, Sodium 349mg, Dietary Fiber 6.7g

String Beans Almondine

1 cup fresh MUSHROOMS, sliced
8 ozs. STRING BEANS, sliced
1 ONION, sliced
1 Tbsp. VEGETABLE OIL
1 tsp. LEMON JUICE
1 Tbsp. TAMARI
dash SPIKE®
dash MARJORAM
1 tsp. THYME
2 Tbsp. ALMONDS, crushed

Steam in covered saucepan, over low heat, all vegetables and spices in 1/2 cup water for 25 minutes. Place vegetables in serving bowl and garnish with almonds. Serves 3.

Per serving: 140 Calories (46% from fat), Protein 4.8g, Carb. 16g, Total Fat 8g, Sodium 1325mg, Dietary Fiber 7.6g

Minted Greens

2 1/2 cups fresh GREEN BEANS, sliced
2 cups TOMATO SAUCE
1 Tbsp. TAMARI
1 tsp. BASIL
1 tsp. MINT
2 Tbsp. ONION, minced
1/2 tsp. OREGANO
1/4 tsp. NUTMEG
1/2 tsp. CINNAMON

Add all ingredients to crockpot and cook covered on low heat for 4 hours.

Serves 4-6.

Per serving: Calories 56 (5% from fat), Protein 3.26g, Carb. 12.7g, Total Fat 0.41g, Sodium 1101mg, Dietary Fiber 2.6g

Shoestring Sweet Potatoes

5 SWEET POTATOES, peeled
2 Tbsp. CANOLA OIL
1 Tbsp. TAMARI
dash SPIKE®

Slice potatoes into shoestring lengths. Lightly oil baking pan and place potatoes on pan. Mix oil, tamari and spike together and brush mixture over potatoes. Bake at 350 degrees for 20 minutes or until done.

Serves 5.

Per serving: Calories 170 (30% from fat), Protein 2.4g, Carb. 28g, Total Fat 5.7g, Sodium 215mg, Dietary Fiber 3.7g

Stuffed Artichokes

4 ARTICHOKES
2 ONIONS, diced
1 Tbsp. TAMARI
1 tsp. GARLIC POWDER
dash BLACK PEPPER
2 Tbsp. VEGETABLE OIL
1/4 cup WALNUTS, finely chopped
3/4 cup WHOLE WHEAT BREAD crumbs

Cut tips of artichokes crosswise. Sauté onions in oil and tamari until soft. Add remaining ingredients to sauté and mix well. Stuff artichokes with the mixture by inserting stuffing between each leaf. Bake stuffed artichokes in a covered baking dish at 350 degrees for 45 minutes to one hour depending on size of artichokes. Artichokes will be soft.

Serves 2-4.

Per serving: Calories 367 (37% from fat), Protein 13.4g, Carb. 50g, Total Fat 16.7g, Sodium 666mg, Dietary Fiber 5.1g

Baked Potato Skins

6 RUSSET BAKING POTATOES   **1 tsp. SPIKE®**
1 Tbsp. VEGETABLE OIL   **1 Tbsp. BASIL**

Bake potatoes at 350 degrees for 1 1/2 hours. Cool and cut each potato in half. Scoop out center and save for another side dish. Oil potato skins and season with spices. Return to oven for 20 minutes till brown and slightly crispy.

Serves 6.

Per serving: Calories 132 (16% from fat), Protein 3.4g, Carb. 25.3g, Total Fat 2.47g, Sodium 203mg, Dietary Fiber 2.8g

Candied Yams

5 YAMS, peeled and cubed
1/4 cup SOY MARGARINE
1/2 cup BROWN RICE SYRUP
1 cup PINEAPPLE, cubed
1 Tbsp. TAMARI
1 tsp. BASIL

Place yams in baking dish. Melt margarine and syrup in small saucepan, add pineapple and tamari to hot mixture and pour over yams. Sprinkle with basil. Bake at 350 degrees for 30-45 minutes until potatoes are soft. Mash and serve.

Serves 4-6.

Per serving: Calories 501 (21% from fat), Protein 4.5g, Carb. 79g, Total Fat 9.7g, Sodium 345mg, Dietary Fiber 0.6g

Broiled Mushrooms

6 lg. MUSHROOMS
2 Tbsp. SOY MARGARINE
1 Tbsp. TAMARI
1 tsp. PARSLEY
dash SPIKE®

Clean mushrooms and remove stems. Place mushrooms cap side down in baking dish. Melt margarine and mix in seasonings. Spoon mixture in center and around mushrooms. Broil until light brown, approximately 7 minutes.

Serves 2.

Per serving: Calories 128 (80% from fat), Protein 2.7g, Carb. 4.14g, Total Fat 11.8g, Sodium 662mg, Dietary Fiber 2.27g

Stuffed Peppers

6 BELL PEPPERS
2 ONIONS, diced
2 Tbsp. OLIVE OIL
1 cup fresh CORN KERNELS
1/2 cup TOMATO, diced
2 cups cooked BROWN RICE
1 Tbsp. TAMARI
1/4 cup WHOLE WHEAT BREAD crumbs

Cut tops off peppers and pull out seeds. Steam in covered pot until tender. Sauté onions in oil until transparent. Add corn, tomato, brown rice and tamari to the sauté. Stuff peppers with mixture and cover with bread crumbs. Place peppers in oiled baking dish and bake at 350 degrees for 10 minutes.

Serves 6.

Per serving: Calories 206 (25% from fat), Protein 4.8g, Carb. 36g, Total Fat 6.1g, Sodium 215mg, Dietary Fiber 5.8g

Candied Carrots

2 cups CARROTS, sliced
1 cup WATER
3 Tbsp. SOY MARGARINE
1 Tbsp. TAMARI

2 Tbsp. BROWN RICE SYRUP
1 Tbsp. BASIL

Steam carrots in water in saucepan until tender, drain and place in baking dish. Melt margarine in saucepan and add remaining ingredients. Pour mixture over carrots and bake at 350 degrees for about 5 minutes.

Serves 3.

Per serving: Calories 175 (72% from fat), Protein 1.58g, Carb. 8.7g, Total Fat 11.7g, Sodium 513mg, Dietary Fiber 0.76g

Deep-Fried Tofu & Vegetables

1 (12 oz.) TOFU CAKE, cut in 1/2-inch cubes
3 cups PEANUT OIL
2 ONIONS, sliced
8 ozs. fresh MUSHROOMS, sliced
3 CARROTS, diced
1 GREEN PEPPER, sliced
1 1/2 Tbsp. TAMARI
1 Tbsp. GINGER ROOT, grated

Deep fry tofu cubes in oil until golden brown. Sauté vegetables and seasonings until tender. Stir tofu into vegetables. Serves 3-4.

Per serving: Calories 366 (48% from fat), Protein 15.3g, Carb. 34.7g, Total Fat 20.7g, Sodium 549mg, Dietary Fiber 6g

Colorful Cabbage Salad

1 cup RED CABBAGE, shredded
1 cup GREEN CABBAGE, shredded
1 RED BELL PEPPER, diced
1 GREEN BELL PEPPER, diced
3 GREEN ONIONS, chopped
3/4 cup VEGETABLE STOCK
4 Tbsp. BROWN RICE VINEGAR
1/2 tsp. MUSTARD
1/2 tsp. BLACK PEPPER

Place all vegetables in large salad bowl. Mix and blend vegetable stock and seasonings to make dressing. Combine all together in bowl, mixing thoroughly. Serves 4-5.

Per serving: Calories 59 (5% from fat), Protein 1.46g, Carb. 13.6g, Total Fat 0.33g, Sodium 20mg, Dietary Fiber 2.94g

Spinach Stuffed Potatoes

6 RUSSET BAKING POTATOES
2 med. ONIONS
3 Tbsp. VEGETABLE OIL
1 bunch SPINACH, stems removed
2 GREEN ONIONS, diced
1/2 tsp. PAPRIKA
1 tsp. PARSLEY
dash SEA SALT

Bake potatoes until done. Cut in half, scoop out center and mash in a bowl. Sauté onions in oil until transparent then add spinach and spices. Cover and simmer for 5 minutes or until spinach is soft. Add sauté to mashed potatoes and fill potato skins with mixture. Place filled potatoes on oiled baking sheet and sprinkle with paprika. Broil for 3-5 minutes until lightly brown on top.

Serves 6.

Per serving: Calories 191 (32% from fat), Protein 4.8g, Carb. 29g, Total Fat 7.1g, Sodium 39mg, Dietary Fiber 4.3g

Marinated Vegetables

1 cup cooked LIMA BEANS
1 cup SNOW PEAS
1 cup BROCCOLI, chopped
1 cup CARROTS, diced
1 cup ZUCCHINI, diced
1/3 cup CANOLA OIL

3 Tbsp. LEMON JUICE
1/8 tsp. BLACK PEPPER
1 Tbsp. TAMARI
1 tsp. BASIL
1 tsp. ONION POWDER
1/4 tsp. DILL WEED

Steam vegetables until soft, add lima beans and vegetables to salad bowl. Combine all other ingredients to make marinade. Pour marinade over vegetables and beans, cover and chill for at least 2 hours. Even better the next day. Serves 4-6.

Per serving: Calories 210 (62% from fat), Protein 5.8g, Carb. 15g, Total Fat 15.3g, Sodium 230mg, Dietary Fiber 5.3g

Special Fried Rice

4 dried SHITAKE
    MUSHROOMS
1 sm. ONION, diced
1 sm. CARROT, diced
1 Tbsp. TAMARI
1 Tbsp. MIRIN

dash SEA SALT
4 SCALLIONS, diced
2 cups BROWN
    RICE, cooked
2 ozs. SNOW PEAS,
    cooked

Cover mushrooms with water and soak until soft, then slice. Sauté onion, carrot and mushrooms until soft. Add tamari, mirin, spices and scallions and continue to sauté for 3 minutes. Add rice and peas, mixing ingredients well, cover and cook for 2 more minutes. Serves 4.

Per serving: Calories 164 (5% from fat), Protein 5.2g, Carb. 35.6g, Total Fat 0.86g, Sodium 273mg, Dietary Fiber 4.8g

Steamed Greens

BROCCOLI FLORETS from 1 stalk
4 ozs. BRUSSELS SPROUTS
1/4 head CABBAGE, shredded
2 cups WATER
1/2 cup SOY MARGARINE
1 Tbsp. TAMARI
1 Tbsp. NUTRITIONAL YEAST

Steam broccoli and brussels sprouts in covered saucepan on low heat till tender. Add cabbage and continue steaming until cabbage is soft. Drain and place in bowl. Melt margarine, add remaining ingredients and pour over vegetables. Serves 4.

Per serving: Calories 241 (82% from fat), Protein 2.9g, Carb. 8.6g, Total Fat 23.3g, Sodium 584mg, Dietary Fiber 2g

Greens & Carrots

3 Tbsp. VEGETABLE OIL
2 CARROTS, grated
2 dried RED CHILI PEPPERS
2 GARLIC CLOVES, minced
4 qts. WATER
1 bunch SWISS CHARD
1 bunch COLLARD GREENS
1 tsp. LEMON JUICE
dash SEA SALT
dash BLACK PEPPER

Sauté carrots, chili peppers and garlic for 3-4 minutes, set aside. Bring water to boil and cook chard and collards for 5 minutes until tender. Drain and squeeze out water. Mix all ingredients together thoroughly in bowl. Serves 4.

Per serving: Calories 133 (67% from fat), Protein 2.66g, Carb. 9.1g, Total Fat 10.5g, Sodium 100mg, Dietary Fiber 2.74g

Sweet Cucumber

1/4 cup BROWN
    RICE VINEGAR
1 Tbsp. SORGHUM
3 Tbsp. TAMARI
1 tsp. FRESH GINGER,
    grated

1/8 cup WATER
2 CUCUMBERS, sliced
1 CARROT, shredded
3 GREEN ONIONS, diced
2 Tbsp. BASIL

Mix vinegar, sorghum, tamari, ginger and water, blend well. Add remainder of ingredients to bowl and pour the vinegar mixture over the vegetables. Cover the bowl and chill for 3 hours. Serves 6.

Per serving: Calories 36 (6% from fat), Protein 1.73g, Carb. 8g, Total Fat 0.25g, Sodium 514mg, Dietary Fiber 0.5g

Spinach Quiche

1 WHOLE WHEAT UNBAKED 8" PIE SHELL
    (see page 104)
1 ONION, diced
3 Tbsp. VEGETABLE OIL
1 med. bunch SPINACH
2 Tbsp. TAMARI
1 (12 oz.) TOFU CAKE, mashed
3 Tbsp. LEMON JUICE
1 Tbsp. DRY MUSTARD
1 tsp. GARLIC POWDER
dash BLACK PEPPER

Sauté onion in oil until translucent. Add spinach and tamari, cover and simmer until spinach is soft. In bowl, mash tofu, add all seasonings and sauté, mixing well. Put mixture into pie shell and bake for 1 hour. Serves 6.

Per serving: 281 Calories (63% from fat), Protein 10g, Carb. 17g, Total Fat 20.7g, Sodium 1059mg, Dietary Fiber 3.8g

Stuffed Mushrooms

8 ozs. lg. MUSHROOMS
4 Tbsp. CANOLA OIL
1/2 cup ONION, finely
   chopped
1 cup WHOLE WHEAT
   BREAD Crumbs

2 tsp. TAMARI
1 tsp. OREGANO
1.tsp. GARLIC POWDER
1/8 tsp. BLACK PEPPER
1 tsp. BASIL

Clean mushrooms, remove stems, brush mushroom caps with oil and place on baking sheet. Chop stems of mushrooms fine and sauté in oil with onion for about 3-4 minutes. Add remaining ingredients to sauté and cook over medium heat for another 3 minutes, stirring occasionally. Spoon sauté mixture into mushroom caps and bake at 350 degrees for 10 minutes. Serves 4.

Per serving: 250 Calories (55% from fat), Protein 5.2g, Carb. 23.6g, Total Fat 15.6g, Sodium 357mg, Dietary Fiber 2.8g

Glazed Squash

2 Tbsp. SOY MARGARINE
1 Tbsp. BROWN RICE
   SYRUP
1 Tbsp. TAMARI
1 tsp. CINNAMON

1 Tbsp. BASIL
1/4 tsp. NUTMEG
1/8 tsp. SPIKE®
3 ACORN SQUASH

Preheat oven 350 degrees. Melt margarine and syrup in small pan, add spices to margarine mixture. Cut squash in half, scoop out seeds. Fill baking pan with 2 inches of water and place squash in pan. Pour margarine mixture into center of squash. Bake till tender 50-55 minutes. Serves 6.

Per serving: 75 Calories (27% from fat), Protein 16.4g, Carb. 8.3g, Total Fat 4g, Sodium 245mg, Dietary Fiber 1g

Onion-Tomato-Tofu Marinade

Marinade:

1 cup WATER
2 tsp. MARJORAM
2 GARLIC CLOVES, diced
1/2 cup OLIVE OIL
1/2 cup BROWN RICE VINEGAR
1/2 cup TAMARI
4 WHOLE CLOVES
1/2 tsp. SEA SALT
dash PEPPER

Other Ingredients:

4 dried SHITAKE MUSHROOMS
1 ONION, sliced
2 TOMATOES, cubed
1 firm (12 oz.) TOFU CAKE, drained, cubed

Prepare marinade in bowl. Cover mushrooms with water and soak until soft and add with other ingredients to marinade. Place bowl in refrigerator and let marinate for 1 day.

Serves 4.

Per serving: 374 Calories (74% from fat), Protein 13g, Carb. 13.2g, Total Fat 33g, Sodium 2312mg, Dietary Fiber 1.85g

Cooked Green Salad

1 ONION, sliced
1 Tbsp. VEGETABLE OIL
2 lbs. KALE, chopped
1 lb. KOHLRABI, chopped
1 lb. LEEKS, chopped

2 Tbsp. TAMARI
1 tsp. GARLIC POWDER
1 tsp. BASIL
1 tsp. PARSLEY
1/4 cup MARGARINE

Slightly sauté onion in oil in saucepan. Add 1 cup water and greens. Cook over low heat until tender. Add remaining ingredients, cover and simmer for 5 more minutes.

Serves 4.

Per serving: 274 Calories (48% from fat), Protein 8.2g, Carb. 30g, Total Fat 16g, Sodium 732mg, Dietary Fiber 1.46g

Steamed Medley

1/2 cup VEGETABLE STOCK or WATER
1 lb. fresh BRUSSELS SPROUTS
3 ASPARAGUS STALKS, chopped
1 sm. EGGPLANT, peeled, diced
1 CARROT, diced
2 GARLIC CLOVES, minced
8 ozs. fresh MUSHROOMS, sliced
1 ONION, diced
FLORETS of 1 stalk BROCCOLI
1 tsp. SAGE
1 tsp. MARJORAM

Place 1/2 cup vegetable stock or water in large saucepan. Add all ingredients and cook covered over low heat for about 30 minutes.

Serves 4.

Per serving: Calories 114 (8% from fat), Protein 7.1g, Carb. 25g, Total Fat 1.27g, Sodium 54mg, Dietary Fiber 7.2g

Rainbow Macaroni Stir

4 cups VEGETABLE MACARONI, cooked
1 GREEN PEPPER, chopped
1 lg. CUCUMBER, peeled, diced
3 TOMATOES
1/4 cup VEGETABLE OIL
1/8 cup BROWN RICE VINEGAR
1/2 cup SOY MAYONNAISE
1 Tbsp. PARSLEY
dash VEGE SAL®
1 Tbsp. MILD MUSTARD
2 Tbsp. RICE SYRUP

Place macaroni, green pepper and cucumber in large bowl. Add tomatoes and all remaining ingredients in blender and blend until smooth. Pour blended mixture over macaroni mixture and stir until well blended. Chill and serve.

Serves 6.

Per serving: 445 Calories (51% from fat), Protein 7g, Carb. 46g, Total Fat 24.6g, Sodium 166mg, Dietary Fiber 4.3g

Vegetable Egg Rolls

1 1/2 Tbsp. VEGETABLE OIL
1/2 tsp. GINGER
1 CELERY STALK, diced
1/2 sm. ONION, diced
1 CARROT, grated
1 cup BEAN SPROUTS
1 tsp. ARROWROOT
1 Tbsp. TAMARI
dash FRUCTOSE
1 package EGGLESS EGG ROLL WRAPS

Heat oil in skillet, stir fry all ingredients 3-5 minutes. Cool mixture and place 1 heaping tablespoon into each egg roll wrap. Fold in sides and roll. Seal with water or sauce. Deep fry for 3-5 minutes until lightly brown.

Serves 8.

Per serving: 59 Calories (39% from fat), Protein 1.8g, Carb. 7.4g, Total Fat 2.6g, Sodium 154mg, Dietary Fiber 0.67g

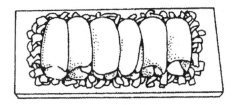

TREATS

Apple Loaf Cake

1/2 cup VEGETABLE OIL
1 1/2 cups DATE SUGAR
1/2 tsp. SEA SALT
2 cups WHOLE WHEAT PASTRY FLOUR
2 tsp. BAKING POWDER
2 lg. APPLES, peeled, chopped
1/2 cup APPLESAUCE
1 cup chopped WALNUTS
1 cup CURRANTS
1 Tbsp. VANILLA
1/2 Tbsp. SORGHUM
3 Tbsp. APPLE JUICE
1 cup COCONUT FLAKES

Mix oil and sugar in large bowl. Sift dry ingredients and mix into oil and sugar. Add remaining ingredients and mix thoroughly. Bake in oiled loaf pan at 350 degrees for 30-45 minutes. Garnish with coconut flakes.

Serves 6.

Per serving: 752 Calories (41% from fat), Protein 11.3g, Carb. 103g, Total Fat 35.4g, Sodium 376mg, Dietary Fiber 8g

Fig & Date Jamboree Cake

1/3 cup VEGETABLE OIL
3/4 cup DATE SUGAR
1 3/4 cups WHOLE WHEAT
    PASTRY FLOUR
1 1/4 cup WATER
1/8 cup RAISINS
1/2 cup DATES, chopped
1/2 cup FIGS, chopped
1/2 cup ALMONDS,
    chopped
1/2 tsp. SEA SALT
1 tsp. BAKING SODA
1 tsp. CINNAMON
1/2 tsp. NUTMEG
2 Tbsp. SORGHUM

Mix oil and sugar in large bowl. Sift in flour, add water, fruit and nuts and mix well. Add remaining ingredients and blend. Place mixture in oiled baking loaf pan and bake at 350 degrees for 35 minutes.

Serves 6-8.

Per slice: 412 Calories (34% from fat), Protein 6.2g, Carb. 65g, Total Fat 16g, Sodium 340mg, Dietary Fiber 6.2g

Carrot Cake

3 Tbsp. VEGETABLE OIL
1 cup PINEAPPLE JUICE
2 cups WHOLE WHEAT
    PASTRY FLOUR
1 cup BROWN RICE
    SYRUP
3/4 cup WATER
2 tsp. VANILLA
1/2 tsp. SEA SALT
1/2 tsp. CINNAMON
1/4 tsp. NUTMEG
1 tsp. grated LEMON RIND
1 1/2 cups grated CARROTS
1/2 cup chopped WALNUTS
1/8 cup RAISINS

Combine all ingredients in large bowl and mix thoroughly. Pour mixture in oiled 8-inch square cake pan and bake 55 minutes.

Serves 6-8.

Per slice: Calories 385 (38% from fat), Protein 7.2g, Carb. 35g, Total Fat 11.6g, Sodium 174mg, Dietary Fiber 4.6g

Single 9-inch Pie Crust

1 cup WHOLE WHEAT PASTRY FLOUR
2 Tbsp. BAKING POWDER
1 tsp. SEA SALT
1/2 tsp. ORANGE JUICE
1/2 cup SOY MARGARINE
1 tsp. VANILLA
2 Tbsp. cold WATER

Combine sifted flour and baking powder. Add liquid ingredients, margarine, salt and vanilla. Mix thoroughly, work dough in hands to form soft ball. Roll on floured wax paper to desired size. Press dough into pie pan. For baked shell prick sides and bottom with fork and bake at 350 degrees for 20 minutes.

Per slice: Calories 154 (67% from fat), Protein 2g, Carb. 11.1g, Total Fat 11.7g, Sodium 755mg, Dietary Fiber 1.63g

Pistachio Chiffon Pie

1 baked PIE CRUST*
3 (8 oz.) TOFU CAKES
10 PISTACHIO NUTS,
   unsalted, ground
1/4 cup BROWN RICE
   SYRUP
2 Tbsp. VANILLA
1/2 tsp. CINNAMON
1/2 tsp. NUTMEG
2 Tbsp. LEMON JUICE
1/2 tsp. SEA SALT
1/8 cup VEGETABLE OIL

*See pie crust recipe above. Combine all ingredients in blender and blend until smooth. Pour mixture in pie shell and bake at 350 degrees for 20 minutes. Cool and serve.

Serves 8.

Per slice: Calories 339 (67% from fat), Protein 11.9g, Carb. 15.7g, Total Fat 23.7g, Sodium 972mg, Dietary Fiber 1.79g

Blueberry Pie

1 UNBAKED PIE CRUST*
1 qt. fresh BLUEBERRIES
4 Tbsp. WHOLE WHEAT
FLOUR
3/4 cup DATE SUGAR

1 Tbsp. SORGHUM
1/2 tsp. CINNAMON
3 Tbsp. COCONUT
FLAKES

*See pie crust recipe page 104. Set coconut flakes aside. Mix well all other ingredients into large bowl. Pour into unbaked pie shell and bake at 350 degrees for 40-45 minutes. Garnish with coconut flakes. Serves 8.

Per slice: Calories 347 (42% from fat), Protein 3.47g, Carb. 51.1g, Total Fat 15.56g,
Sodium 788.40mg, Dietary Fiber 6.03g

Peach Walnut Pie

Double unbaked PIE CRUST*
3 1/2 cups sliced fresh PEACHES
1/2 cup chopped DATES
1/2 cup PEACH JUICE
1/4 tsp. CORIANDER
2 Tbsp. WHOLE WHEAT FLOUR
1/4 cup WALNUTS, ground

*See pie crust recipe page 104. Simmer fruit and juice for 5 minutes until fruit softens. Slowly add remaining ingredients, stirring to blend well. Use 1/2 of pie crust recipe to form pie shell. Pour in peach mixture. Roll out other 1/2 of pie crust recipe to form top for pie. Cut slits and lay over pie. Pinch to seal sides. Trim excess and bake at 350 degrees for 30 minutes until lightly browned. Serves 8.

Per slice: Calories 251 (44% from fat), Protein 3.9g, Carb. 30.6g, Total Fat 14.1g, Sodium 756mg, Dietary Fiber 4.53g

Strawberry Cream Pie

1 baked PIE CRUST*
1 Tbsp. APPLE JUICE
1/2 cup VEGETABLE OIL
1 cup DATE SUGAR
1/4 cup RICE SYRUP
1/4 tsp. SEA SALT
2 (12 oz.) TOFU CAKES
1 cup sliced fresh STRAWBERRIES
1/8 cup COCONUT FLAKES

*See pie crust recipe page 104. Set strawberries and coconut flakes aside. Combine all other ingredients in blender and blend until smooth and creamy. Gently fold in strawberries and pour into pie shell. Garnish with coconut flakes. Chill for 4 hours.

Serves 8.

Per cup: Calories 395 (72% from fat), Protein 9.9, Carb. 16.1g, Total Fat 30.9g, Sodium 842mg, Dietary Fiber 2.16g

Carob Mousse Pie

1 baked PIE CRUST*	3/4 cup OIL
1 tsp. AGAR-AGAR	1 cup DATE SUGAR
1 tsp. ARROWROOT	1/2 cup BROWN RICE
1 Tbsp. TAHINI	SYRUP
3/4 cup CAROB	2 tsp. VANILLA
1/4 tsp. SEA SALT	3/4 cup WATER
3 cups TOFU	3 Tbsp. chopped PECANS

*See pie crust recipe page 104. Set pecans aside. Bring water to a boil, and slowly stir in agar-agar, arrowroot, salt, tahini and carob. Continue stirring until mixture is well blended. Lower heat and simmer for 15 minutes, stirring occasionally. Cool for 45 minutes. Add remaining ingredients to cooled mixture, stirring until mixture is smooth. Pour into pie crust and bake at 350 degrees for 20 minutes. Garnish with pecans. Chill and serve. Serves 8.

Per slice: Calories 508 (68% from fat), Protein 10.9g, Carb. 32g, Total Fat 39.4g, Sodium 860mg, Dietary Fiber 2.9g

Tofu Cheese Cake

1 baked PIE CRUST*	1/4 cup BROWN RICE
1 Tbsp. roasted ALMOND	SYRUP
SLIVERS	1/2 tsp. SEA SALT
3 (8 oz.) TOFU CAKES	1 tsp. VANILLA
1/3 cup LEMON JUICE	1/4 tsp. NUTMEG
3/4 cup DATE SUGAR	

*See pie crust recipe page 104. Set almonds aside. Combine all other ingredients in blender and blend until smooth and creamy. Pour into pie shell and bake at 350 degrees for 30 minutes. Garnish with almonds. Chill and serve. Serves 8.

Per slice: Calories 262 (60% from fat), Protein 9.9g, Carb. 13.8g, Total Fat 16.7g, Sodium 912mg, Dietary Fiber 1.86g

Fruit Roll

Pastry dough:

1 cup WHOLE WHEAT PASTRY FLOUR
2 Tbsp. BAKING POWDER
1/2 cup SOY MARGARINE
1 tsp. SEA SALT
1/2 tsp. ORANGE JUICE
1 Tbsp. VANILLA
2 Tbsp. cold WATER

Sift flour and baking powder together. Melt margarine and add to flour along with remaining ingredients, mixing thoroughly. Work dough into a soft ball. Roll on floured wax paper into a rectangular shape.

Filling:

2 cups RAISINS
2 1/2 cups FIGS, chopped
1 cup chopped WALNUTS
3/4 cup ORANGE JUICE
1/2 cup LEMON JUICE
1 LEMON RIND, grated
1 cup COCONUT FLAKES
1 Tbsp. VANILLA
1 Tbsp. BROWN RICE SYRUP
1/2 Tbsp. DATE SUGAR

Mix all filling ingredients together in large bowl, blending thoroughly. Spread filling on dough leaving 1-inch border. Cover border with syrup. Gently roll, using syrup to seal the seam. Press in ends. Bake at 350 degrees for 45 minutes. When cool, slice into desired serving size.

Serves 8-10.

Per slice: Calories 546 (42% from fat), Protein 8.1g, Carb. 74g, Total Fat 27g, Sodium 750mg, Dietary Fiber 6.4g

Banana-Nut Bread

Mix in a bowl:

1 (8 oz.) TOFU CAKE, mashed
1 1/4 cups mashed BANANA
1/2 cup DATE SUGAR
1/2 cup BROWN RICE SYRUP
1 Tbsp. ORANGE JUICE
1 tsp. VANILLA
1/8 tsp. CINNAMON
1/4 tsp. SEA SALT

In another bowl mix:

2 cups WHOLE WHEAT
   FLOUR
1/2 tsp. BAKING POWDER
1/2 tsp. BAKING SODA
1 tsp. SOY POWDER

Add:

1/4 cup RAISINS
3/4 cup BRAZIL NUTS, chopped

Combine moist and dry ingredients and mix thoroughly. Add nuts and raisins. Oil loaf baking pan and pour in mixture. Bake at 350 degrees for 1 hour. Test middle with toothpick; if still too moist, bake an additional 10 minutes.

Yields one loaf (12 slices).

Per slice: Calories 261 (31% from fat), Protein 7.8g, Carb. 33.3g, Total Fat 8.2g, Sodium 104mg, Dietary Fiber 4g

Walnut-Coconut Cookies

1/2 cup WHOLE WHEAT FLOUR
1/8 cup crushed WALNUTS
4 Tbsp. VEGETABLE OIL
3/4 cup DATE SUGAR
2 Tbsp. RICE SYRUP
1/2 tsp. SEA SALT
1 Tbsp. ORANGE JUICE
1/2 tsp. LEMON JUICE
1/4 tsp. VANILLA
1 1/2 cup shredded COCONUT

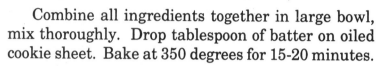

Combine all ingredients together in large bowl, mix thoroughly. Drop tablespoon of batter on oiled cookie sheet. Bake at 350 degrees for 15-20 minutes.

Yields 1 dozen cookies.

Per cookie: Calories 181 (48% from fat), Protein 1.33g, Carb. 21.4g, Total Fat 9.5g, Sodium 125mg, Dietary Fiber 0.68g

Baked Apple Supreme

4 lg. ROME APPLES
1 cup APPLE JUICE
1/2 cup RAISINS

1 Tbsp. BROWN RICE
   SYRUP
dash CINNAMON

Cut 1/4 inch from top of apples and core. Combine 1/2 juice, raisins and syrup and fill centers of apples. Place in baking dish and sprinkle cinnamon over apples. Pour other 1/2 of juice in baking dish around the apples. Bake at 350 degrees for 45 minutes. Spoon apple juice over apples every 10 minutes. Cool and serve.

Serves 4.

Per apple: Calories 218 (4% from fat), Protein 1.08g, Carb. 53g, Total Fat 0.9g, Sodium 5.4mg, Dietary Fiber 6.2g

Strawberry Sherbet

1/2 cup DATE SUGAR
1/3 cup WATER
2 1/2 cups STRAWBERRIES

Boil water and add sugar until dissolved. Let it cool and add to blender with strawberries and blend until smooth. Refrigerate until cool. Serves 2-3.

Per cup: Calories 248 (3% from fat), Protein 1.12g, Carb. 61g, Total Fat 0.75g, Sodium 4.3mg, Dietary Fiber 3.75g

Papaya-Lime Tropical

2 cups PAPAYA PULP
1 Tbsp. LIME JUICE
1/2 cup fresh ORANGE JUICE
1 Tbsp. BROWN RICE SYRUP
2 Tbsp. COCONUT FLAKES

Set coconut flakes aside. Combine all ingredients into food processor until smooth and creamy. Add mixture to sherbet glasses. Garnish with coconut flakes. Refrigerate 2 hours. Serves 4.

Per cup: Calories 192 (44% from fat), Protein 1.6g, Carb. 24.6g, Total Fat 9.3g, Sodium 75mg, Dietary Fiber 1.26g

Crenshaw Freeze

3 cups CRENSHAW MELON
1 cup ORANGE JUICE
1 frozen BANANA
2 Tbsp. SORGHUM

Scoop out crenshaw pulp to make 3 cups. Add all ingredients to food processor until creamy and smooth. Pour into sherbet glasses. Freeze for 3 hours. Serves 4.

Per cup: Calories 180 (2% from fat), Protein 3.1g, Carb. 43g, Total Fat 0.46g, Sodium 37mg, Dietary Fiber 4.1g

Pineapple Gelatin

1/2 cup WATER
2 tsp. AGAR-AGAR
3 Tbsp. SORGHUM
2 Tbsp. COCONUT MEAL
1 cup sliced fresh PINEAPPLE
1 cup STRAWBERRIES
1/4 cup COCONUT JUICE
1/4 cup BANANAS, sliced

Boil water with agar-agar, add sorghum, coconut meal, pineapple, strawberries, juice and water to blender and blend until smooth. Pour into dessert dishes and add banana slices. Chill for 2 hours.

Serves 4.

Per cup: Calories 195 (12% from fat), Protein 2g, Carb. 62g, Total Fat 3.7g, Sodium 20.6mg, Dietary Fiber 3.1g

Fruit Balls

1 cup DATES, chopped
1 cup FIGS, chopped
3/4 cup CASHEWS, finely chopped
1/3 cup SORGHUM
1/4 cup APPLE JUICE
1 cup COCONUT MEAL

Add all the ingredients in a large bowl and mix thoroughly. Shape small bite-sized balls with fingers and roll into coconut meal. Place on waxed paper and cover with waxed paper. Refrigerate for a day. Great snack for children.

Yields 12-20 fruit balls.

Per cup: Calories 176 (49% from fat), Protein 1.97g, Carb. 22.4g, Total Fat 10.2g, Sodium 48mg, Dietary Fiber 1.74g

Stuffed Prunes

12 lg. PRUNES
2 Tbsp. SUNFLOWER SEEDS, ground
2 Tbsp. APPLE JUICE
4 Tbsp. COCONUT MEAL
1 Tbsp. WALNUTS, ground
1 1/2 Tbsp. SORGHUM

Cover prunes with boiling water and let sit for 20 minutes. Drain prunes and when they have cooled, open each prune and remove pit. Mix other ingredients thoroughly and fill each prune with mixture. Brush prunes with sorghum and roll in coconut meal. Refrigerate 2 hours.

Per prune: Calories 102 (40% from fat), Protein 1.87g, Carb. 14.7g, Total Fat 5g, Sodium 2.1mg, Dietary Fiber 2.86g

Cooked Pears

4 BARTLETT PEARS, peeled,
    cored, sliced
4 Tbsp. APPLE JUICE
1 BANANA
1/2 tsp. CINNAMON
3 Tbsp. RAISINS
1/2 tsp. NUTMEG

Place pears in glass baking dish. In a blender, blend remaining ingredients and pour over pears. Cover baking dish with aluminum wrap and bake at 350 degrees for 15 minutes or until pears are soft. Chill and serve.

Serves 4.

Per cup: Calories 154 (5% from fat), Protein 1.25g, Carb. 39g, Total Fat 1g, Sodium 2.6mg, Dietary Fiber 5.3g

Carob Topping

3/4 cup WATER
1/2 tsp. VANILLA
2 Tbsp. SORGHUM
3 Tbsp. CAROB
1 Tbsp. CASHEW BUTTER
1 Tbsp. SOY POWDER

Place all ingredients in blender and blend until smooth.

Yield 1 cup.

Per 1/4 cup: Calories 52.4 (26% from fat), Protein 1.12g, Carb. 10.2g, Total Fat 1.82g, Sodium 4.65mg, Dietary Fiber 0.76g

Carob Banana Sweets

1 1/2 cups WHOLE WHEAT FLOUR
1 tsp. BAKING POWDER
1/4 tsp. BAKING SODA
1/2 tsp. SEA SALT
3/4 cup WATER
4 BANANAS, peeled
3 cups VEGETABLE OIL
1 cup CAROB TOPPING (see above)

Mix 1 cup flour, baking powder, baking soda and salt in bowl. Add water slowly and mix until smooth to form batter. Cut bananas in quarters. Roll each quarter in remaining 1/2 cup flour and then roll in batter. Deep fry for 5 minutes or until golden brown. Let cool and dip into carob topping.

Serves 4-6.

Per cup: Calories 1409.4 (85% from fat), Protein 6.9g, Carb. 57g, Total Fat 133.8g, Sodium 359mg, Dietary Fiber 7.06g

Banana Ice Cream

6 frozen BANANAS   **1/2 cup CAROB TOPPING***
1/3 cup PEANUT BUTTER **3 Tbsp. SOY MILK**

*See page 114. Combine all ingredients in food processor and blend until smooth and creamy. Pour into dessert dishes and freeze for 2-3 hours. Serves 4.

Per cup: Calories 340 (30% from fat), Protein 9.22g, Carb. 54.2g, Total Fat 13.8g, Sodium 107.6mg, Dietary Fiber 7g

Carob Float

1 1/2 cup SOY MILK   **1 Tbsp. TAHINI**
1 1/4 Tbsp. INSTANT   **4 Tbsp. BANANA ICE**
   CAROB   **CREAM (see above)**
2 tsp. MAPLE SYRUP

Combine first 4 ingredients in blender and blend until smooth. Add ice cream just before serving. Yields 2 glasses.

Per glass: Calories 213 (44% from fat), Protein 8.7g, Carb. 26.3g, Total Fat 10.9g, Sodium 59.9mg, Dietary Fiber 4.13g

Carob Banana Pops

4 BANANAS, peeled   **1/2 cup crushed NUTS**
4 POPSICLE STICKS   **1/4 cup shredded**
1 cup CAROB TOPPING*   **COCONUT**

*See page 114. Insert stick into each banana, place on baking sheet, cover with plastic wrap and freeze. Remove from freezer and dip first in carob topping, then nuts and coconut. Put back in freezer. Serves 4.

Per cup: Calories 276.4 (38% from fat), Protein 3.5g, Carb. 42.2g, Total Fat 13.6g, Sodium 124.6mg, Dietary Fiber 4.7g

Strawberry Melon Balls

1/2 CANTALOUPE MELON
1/4 HONEYDEW MELON
1/4 CASABA MELON
2 cups STRAWBERRIES
1/2 cup crushed ICE
2 Tbsp. COCONUT FLAKES
2 Tbsp. PISTACHIO NUTS, ground

Form melon balls with a melon ball scoop and place in serving bowl. Add strawberries and crushed ice to blender and blend until smooth. Pour over fruit and garnish with coconut flakes and pistachio nuts. Serve cold.

Serves 4-6.

Per cup: Calories 172 (31% from fat), Protein 3.34g, Carb. 29.4g, Total Fat 6.5g, Sodium 83mg, Dietary Fiber 4g

BEVERAGES

Blackberry Malted

1 cup fresh BLACKBERRIES
1 frozen BANANA
2 cups SOY MILK
1 tsp. SORGHUM

Combine all ingredients in blender and blend until smooth. Yields 2 glasses.

Per glass: Calories 177 (24% from fat), Protein 7.7g, Carb. 29g, Total Fat 5.2g, Sodium 30.5mg, Dietary Fiber 7.4g

Sweet Shake

3/4 cup sliced PEACHES
1/4 cup fresh STRAWBERRIES
1 1/2 cup SOY MILK
1 frozen BANANA
1 tsp. SORGHUM
1 tsp. VANILLA
1/4 cup crushed ICE

Combine all ingredients in a blender and blend until smooth. Yields 2 glasses.

Per glass: Calories 150 (22% from fat), Protein 6g, Carb. 25g, Total Fat 3.9g, Sodium 28mg, Dietary Fiber 4.8

Apricot Smoothie

1 cup APPLE JUICE
1/2 cup APRICOT JUICE
1/2 cup SPARKLING WATER
1 tsp. SORGHUM

1 Tbsp. chopped DATES
1 frozen BANANA

Combine all ingredients in blender and blend until smooth. Yields 2 glasses.

Per glass: Calories 170 (3% from fat), Protein 1.03g, Carb. 43g, Total Fat 0.52g, Sodium 6.4mg, Dietary Fiber 2.37g

Herbal Crispy Apple Spice

6 cups WATER
5 HERBAL CRISPY APPLE TEA BAGS

1 CINNAMON STICK
2 Tbsp. SORGHUM

Bring water to a boil, add tea bags and cinnamon stick. Let simmer about 5 minutes and add sweetener. Yields 5 cups.

Per cup: Calories 22.6 (1% from fat), Protein 0.02g, Carb. 6g, Total Fat 0.02g, Sodium 8.5mg, Dietary Fiber 0g

Pineapple Punch

1 1/2 qts. ICE WATER
1/2 cup FROZEN ORANGE JUICE CONCENTRATE
1/2 cup fresh PINEAPPLE
1 tsp. SORGHUM

Combine all ingredients in a blender and blend until smooth. Garnish with slices of pineapple. Yields 2 quarts.

Per glass: Calories 14 (3% from fat), Protein 0.15g, Carb. 3.5g, Total Fat 0.05g, Sodium 5.4mg, Dietary Fiber 0.13g

Grape Flush

2 cups GRAPE JUICE
1 cup SPARKLING WATER
1 cup SOY MILK
1 frozen BANANA
1/8 cup CRUSHED ICE
1 tsp. SORGHUM

Combine all ingredients in a blender and blend until smooth. Yields 2 glasses.

Per glass: Calories 256 (9% from fat), Protein 5.3g, Carb. 56g, Total Fat 2.8g, Sodium 22.5mg, Dietary Fiber 2.8g

Orange Freeze

1 1/2 cups FRESH ORANGE
    JUICE
1/4 cup SPARKLING WATER
1/8 cup FRESH LIME JUICE
1/8 cup CRUSHED ICE
2 tsp. SORGHUM
1 frozen BANANA
4 lg. STRAWBERRIES

Combine first 6 ingredients in a blender and blend until smooth. Garnish with strawberries. Yields 2 glasses.

Per glass: Calories 169 (4% from fat), Protein 2.17g, Carb. 41.5g, Total Fat 0.84g, Sodium 2.6mg, Dietary Fiber 2.63g

Raspberry Cocktail

1 cup fresh RASPBERRIES
1/2 cup SOY MILK
1 cup ORANGE JUICE
1 tsp. SORGHUM
6 Tbsp. CRUSHED ICE

Combine first 4 ingredients in a blender and blend until smooth. Put 2 tablespoons crushed ice 3 glasses and add mixture.

Per glass: Calories 77 (13% from fat), Protein 2.07g, Carb. 16.3g, Total Fat 1.2g, Sodium 5.7mg, Dietary Fiber 6.7g

Sangria Cocktail

1 1/2 cups CRANBERRY JUICE
1 1/2 tsp. LEMON JUICE
1 3/4 cups SPARKLING WATER
2 Tbsp. SORGHUM
1/8 cup SOY MILK
6 Tbsp. CRUSHED ICE

Combine first 5 ingredients in a blender and blend until smooth. Put 2 tablespoons of ice in 3 glasses and add mixture.

Per glass: Calories 113 (2% from fat), Protein 0.33g, Carb. 28.7g, Total Fat 0.25g, Sodium 6.8mg, Dietary Fiber 0.11g

Vanilla Cooler

1 cup SOY MILK
1 frozen BANANA
2 tsp. SORGHUM
1 Tbsp. shredded COCONUT
1 tsp. VANILLA
2 Tbsp. BANANA ICE CREAM*
1/8 cup CRUSHED ICE

*See recipe page 115. Combine all ingredients in a blender and blend until smooth. Yields 2 glasses.

Per glass: Calories 129 (24% from fat), Protein 4g, Carb. 21.7g, Total Fat 3.6g, Sodium 27.6mg, Dietary Fiber 2.8g

Bloody Mary

2 Tbsp. FRESH LEMON JUICE
1 cup TOMATO JUICE
3/4 cup CELERY JUICE
dash SEA SALT
dash TAMARI
6 Tbsp. CRUSHED ICE

Combine first 5 ingredients in blender and blend until smooth. Put 3 tablespoons of ice in 2 glasses and add mixture. Garnish with lemon slice.

Per glass: Calories 60 (3% from fat), Protein 2.5g, Carb. 12.7g, Total Fat 0.19g, Sodium 354mg, Dietary Fiber 0.86g

Nature's Cocktail

1 cup BEET JUICE
1 cup CELERY JUICE
1/2 cup CARROT JUICE

1 tsp. PARSLEY
6 Tbsp. CRUSHED ICE

Using a juicer, make fresh juice for your cocktail. Add parsley and blend together. Put 2 tablespoons of ice in 3 glasses and add mixture.

Per glass: Calories 79 (7% from fat), Protein 2.4g, Carb. 16.7g, Total Fat 0.6g, Sodium 161mg, Dietary Fiber 0.4g

Tahini Shake

1 1/2 cups WATER
1/2 cup SOY MILK
2 frozen BANANAS

1 1/2 tsp. TAHINI
1 tsp. VANILLA
1 tsp. MAPLE SYRUP

Combine all ingredients in a blender and blend until smooth. Yields 3 glasses.

Per glass: Calories 107 (20% from fat), Protein 2.33g, Carb. 20.6g, Total Fat 2.5g, Sodium 16.4mg, Dietary Fiber 2.43g

Watermelon Smoothie

4 cups WATERMELON,
    pitted
2 frozen BANANAS

1 cup SOY MILK
1/2 cup APPLE JUICE

Combine all ingredients in a blender. Blend until smooth. Yields 4 glasses.

Per glass: Calories 137 (13% from fat), Protein 3.3g, Carb. 29.5g, Total Fat 2.2g, Sodium 11.9mg, Dietary Fiber 3.6g

Nut Milk

1/2 cup hulled SUNFLOWER SEEDS
5 1/2 cups WATER
1/2 cup SOY MILK
1 tsp. MAPLE SYRUP

Blend seeds and 2 cups of water at high speed until smooth and creamy. Slowly add another 2 cups water and soy milk. Blend 1 minute. Add sweetener and remainder of water. Blend another minute until mixture is completely liquified and smooth. Fill pitcher 1/4 full with ice and add nut milk. Refrigerate for at least 1 hour. Great as a drink or over cereal. Yields 6 glasses.

Per glass: Calories 50 (66% from fat), Protein 2.17g, Carb. 2.4g, Total Fat 3.9g, Sodium 9.3mg, Dietary Fiber 0.52g

Peach Melba

1 cup PEACHES
1/2 cup RASPBERRIES
1/2 cup SOY MILK
1 tsp. SORGHUM
6 Tbsp. CRUSHED ICE

Combine all ingredients in a blender and blend until smooth. Yields 2 glasses.

Per glass: Calories 81 (14% from fat), Protein 2.55g, Carb. 17g, Total Fat 1.45g, Sodium 7.5mg, Dietary Fiber 7.2g

Morning Coffee Substitute

1 cup WATER
1 tsp. KAFFREE ROMA®
2 Tbsp. SOY MILK
1 tsp. RICE SYRUP

Pour boiling water in cup. Add coffee substitute and soy milk. Stir in sweetener. Yields 1 cup.

Per cup: Calories 28 (49% from fat), Protein 0.83g, Carb. 0.54g, Total Fat 0.58g, Sodium 10.7mg, Dietary Fiber 0.33g

Index

Meet the Author

Chef Morty Star has been a vegetarian for almost 25 years. He spent many years experimenting with sprout diets, fruitarian diets, raw food diets and juice regimens to creat this collection of purely vegetarian recipes.

He believes passionately that the consumption of animal fats is harmful to good health.

Morty and his "soul mate and partner" Norma Jean, live in Lutz, Florida.

References

1. Surgeon General's Report on Diet and Health, 1989, U.S. Government Printing Office.1. Theusen, L. Beneficial effect of a low-fat, low-calorie diet on myocardial energy metabolism in patients with angina pectoris. Lancet 2:59, 1984.

2. Stamler, J. Prevention and control of hypertension by nutritional-hygienic means: long term experience of the Chicago Coronary Convention Evaluation Program. JAMA, 243:1819, 1980.

3. Simpson, R. Improved glucose control in maturity-onset diabetes treated with high-carbohydrate modified diet. British Medical Journal, 1:1753, 1979.

Simpson, H. A high-carbohydrate leguminous fiber diet improves all aspects of diabetic control. Lancet 1:1, 1981.

4. De Waard, F. (1986.) Dietary fat and mammary cancer. Nutr. and Cancer, 8(1), 5-8.

5. Hill, P. Diet, Life-Style, and Menstrual Activity. American Journal of Clinical Nutrition, 33:1192, 1980.

Reddy, B.S., et al. Nutrition and its Relationship to Cancer Research, 41:3817, 1981.

6. Hill, P. Environmental Factors of Breasts and Prostatic Cancer. Cancer Research, 41:3817, 1981.

7. Van Faassen, et al. Bile acids, neutral steroids, and bacteria in feces as affected by a mixed, a lacto-vegetarian, and a vegan diet. Am. J. Clin. Nutr., 46, 962-967, 1987.

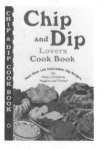

ORDER BLANK

GOLDEN WEST PUBLISHERS

☼ 4113 N. Longview Ave. • Phoenix, AZ 85014

602-265-4392 • **1-800-658-5830** • FAX 602-279-6901

Qty	Title	Price	Amount
	Apple-Lovers' Cook Book	6.95	
	Arizona Cook Book	5.95	
	California Favorites Cook Book	5.95	
	Chip and Dip Lovers Cook Book	5.95	
	Christmas in Arizona Cook Book	8.95	
	Christmas in New Mexico Cook Book	8.95	
	Citrus Lovers Cook Book	6.95	
	Colorado Favorites Cook Book	5.95	
	Date Recipes	6.95	
	Joy of Muffins	5.95	
	Mexican Desserts & Drinks	6.95	
	New Mexico Cook Book	5.95	
	Pecan-Lovers' Cook Book	6.95	
	Pumpkin Recipes	6.95	
	Quick-n-Easy Mexican Recipes	5.95	
	Recipes for a Healthy Lifestyle	6.95	
	Salsa Lovers Cook Book	5.95	
	Texas Cook Book	5.95	
	Veggie Lovers Cook Book	6.95	
Add $2.00 to total order for shipping & handling			**$2.00**

☐ My Check or Money Order Enclosed. . . . . $

☐ MasterCard   ☐ VISA

Acct. No.   Exp. Date

Signature

Name   Telephone

Address

City/State/Zip

Call for FREE catalog

Veggie

3/94

MasterCard and VISA Orders Accepted ($20 Minimum)

This order blank may be photo-copied.